A Spear-Carrier
in Viet Nam

A Spear-Carrier in Viet Nam

Memoir of an American Civilian in Country, 1967 and 1970–1972

MICHAEL E. TOLLE

McFarland & Company, Inc., Publishers

Jefferson, North Carolina

All photographs are from the author's collection.

LIBRARY OF CONGRESS CATALOGUING-IN-PUBLICATION DATA

Names: Tolle, Michael E., 1947– author.
Title: A spear-carrier in Viet Nam : memoir of an American civilian in country, 1967 and 1970–1972 / Michael E. Tolle.
Other titles: Memoir of an American civilian in country, 1967 and 1970–1972
Description: Jefferson, North Carolina : McFarland & Company, Inc., Publishers, 2018 | Includes bibliographical references and index.
Identifiers: LCCN 2018045018 | ISBN 9781476675978 (softcover : acid free paper) ∞
Subjects: LCSH: Tolle, Michael E., 1947– | Vietnam War, 1961–1975—Civilian relief—Biography. | United States. Military Assistance Command, Vietnam. Civil Operations and Rural Development Support—Officials and employees—Biography. | USAID/Vietnam—Officials and employees—Biography. | Diplomats—United States—Biography. | Vietnam War, 1961–1975—War work. | Vietnam—Description and travel. | Vietnam War, 1961–1975—Refugees. | Vietnam War, 1961–1975—Personal narratives, American.
Classification: LCC DS557 .T65 2018 | DDC 959.704/31 [B]—dc23
LC record available at https://lccn.loc.gov/2018045018

BRITISH LIBRARY CATALOGUING DATA ARE AVAILABLE

ISBN (print) 978-1-4766-7597-8
ISBN (ebook) 978-1-4766-3438-8

The front cover image is of Michael Tolle at the intersection of routes I and 9, in Quang Tri Province, just south of the DMZ, summer 1967

Printed in the United States of America

McFarland & Company, Inc., Publishers
  Box 611, Jefferson, North Carolina 28640
  www.mcfarlandpub.com

To Nguyen van Trong and his family,
and by extension, to all those who bought
into our promises but were left behind

Table of Contents

Preface

The memories in this book focus on Viet Nam, so I will be brief with the earlier details. Yet Viet Nam was, for me, a transformational experience, and thus requires some context.

I was born in Kansas in 1947, an early baby boomer. My father pursued education as a graduate student, and the family—I was the oldest of three boys—moved to Michigan before I could form any real memories of Kansas. These were hard times, as my father did not qualify for veterans' benefits under the GI Bill. Bad eyes had rendered him 4F, but like every other young man he still wanted to do his part, so once he turned 18 he joined the Merchant Marine. He shipped out of San Francisco, and on his first voyage his Liberty Ship was hit by a kamikaze in its stern quarter. That was actually fortunate, as the ship's forward hold contained aviation gasoline, but the strike damaged the propeller shaft to the extent that the ship had to return all the way to San Francisco at three knots, a slow and very nervous voyage. Regardless of that, veterans of the Merchant Marine were not considered real veterans, so money was tight for quite some time.

We moved to the Detroit suburbs, while my father earned his EdD at Wayne State University. We then moved to Long Island, and my father began to teach at Brooklyn College, after which he became a public school administrator. We moved to the old but rapidly expanding (at that time) town of East Islip in Suffolk County, about halfway across Long Island's south shore. I did not exactly grow up in a diverse neighborhood. My family lived at three locations in East Islip, with by far the most time spent on Overlook Drive in Country Village. This was a classic housing development of the times, a farm reshaped for streets and lots after being stripped of its vegetation and topsoil. The homes were brand new and offered versions of the colonial style plus a split-level. The only trees on

1

the entire site when the first residents moved in were saplings held up by a pair of stakes driven into the ground next to them. Several homes had spent a lot of money on landscaping, but others hadn't and the contrasts could be striking.

This was strictly a housing development, with no commercial enterprises allowed. It was (and still is) just off Main Street and almost opposite the old high school. There was a small, strip shopping center at the intersection, but pretty much anything else you wanted to do required a car. There were no African American residents in Country Village, of course. Such diversity as I grew up with came from the considerable number of Jewish families who chose to live in the new developments such as mine. There are those who can claim that "some of my best friends are Jewish," but growing up virtually *all* of mine were.

As far back as I can remember I have been intensely interested in what they used to call "current affairs." I have clear mental images of the sinking of the *Andrea Doria* and the time my parents allowed me to stay up to watch the roll call when President Eisenhower was nominated for a second term, both in 1956. Things got serious the next year, and I remember the front page of Long Island's *Newsday*, which announced the launch of Sputnik. That headline read, "Russia Wins Space Race." I was ten years old. I, like many others of greater age, didn't even know that there was a space race, but missiles and rockets were soon the subject of daily headlines, all in the context of the Cold War. We all grew up with that giant shadow over our heads; two fundamentally opposed ideologies, each with the power to destroy not only each other but also pretty much everybody else on the planet, vying for world supremacy. I was one of those who periodically had to march out of my elementary school classroom and line up in the hallway with my hands on the back of my head. It was only later that I realized that should this calamity actually occur the living would envy the dead.

It was during these formative years that I encountered Ayn Rand. The chance reading of a small tract entitled *Anthem* led to a not-atypical adolescent flirtation with "Objectivism." Thus primed, I had by 1963 found my first political hero in the person of Senator Barry Goldwater. Goldwater's *The Conscience of a Conservative* made a deep impression on my recently Ayn Rand–imprinted mind, and together these two led to the long-lasting (if decidedly singular) interpretation of "libertarianism" that has guided my life.

My adolescent discovery of Ayn Rand was followed by my enlistment as one of "Barry's Boys." My first political activism took the form of a bus ride to Washington, D.C., to attend a "Draft Goldwater" rally. Then-popular TV star Efrem Zimbalist, Jr., was the keynote speaker. In 1964 I served as vice chairman of the Suffolk County, Long Island, Youth for Goldwater, which sounds more prestigious than it was. It was just a title, as I performed no actual function. By my high school graduation, I was a libertarian conservative, one of the many in each generation who had become so in the rarified air of white privilege. Privilege in my case had almost everything to do with race. I processed through a public school system that had Jews aplenty but the children of exactly one African-American family.

What had been a minor but growing topic in the news—what was happening in a small country exactly halfway around the world named Viet Nam—when I entered 9th grade in the fall of 1962 grew in both frequency and intensity during my high school years. Questions of support or opposition for our nation's policy aside, we adolescent men had to deal with a very important, very individual issue. "The Draft" became a constant source of thought, although it was almost never mentioned specifically, at least in my circle of "college-bound" students. Those on the "prepare for the workplace" track had to deal with it more earnestly, because they would face it at least four years earlier than any of those who were college bound.

I graduated from high school in 1965, a college acceptance already in hand. Actually, I had more than one but the one I wanted was from the School of Foreign Service at Georgetown University. My fascination with "international relations" had coalesced when a teacher of mine recommended Georgetown, his alma mater. I checked out its catalog and found it to be the school of my dreams. What better place to study international relations than in Washington, D.C.? The School of Foreign Service (SFS) was not just a major but an actual school, with a separate faculty, administration, and campus (unlike today). The fact that I would not be required to take a single math or science course during my four years there pretty much sealed the deal. I set my mind on SFS, applied to the school, and received early admission, but that didn't mean things were settled. My father and my football coach wanted me to attend an Ivy League school and did their best to change my mind. They failed. Georgetown it was.

Still in the thrall of adolescent libertarianism and of the Republican

Preface

"aggressive" policy toward Communism, I supported our involvement in the Viet Nam war when I arrived at Georgetown. My roommate did not, and we went round and round on the subject. The fact that both of us had arrived at our opposite opinions without any actual knowledge of Viet Nam did not occur to either of us, nor to virtually anyone else I encountered, because that's how everyone came to their opinion. That would change, for me at least.

During my freshman year in 1966 came the news that first brought the Viet Nam war home to me. My father called to tell me that he had accepted an appointment with the United States Agency for International Development (USAID) to serve as an education advisor to the Government of the Republic of [South] Viet Nam (GVN). The U.S. government had decided on a policy of rapid increase in the number of civilian advisory personnel in Viet Nam and began to recruit nationally. This was what had attracted my father's attention. A number of men (and a few women), seeing the opportunity for some war-like adventure without the discomfort of a uniform or a gun, signed up. They came from a wide variety of professions, although ex-policemen were probably the largest component. My father, with an EdD, would assist in the much-needed improvement of the country's literacy rate. Dad came to Washington, D.C., for a brief period of orientation before leaving for overseas. I was able to spend a little bit of time with him while he was in D.C. and even managed to attend a couple of the talks given to him and his fellow AID recruits. This included a fascinating—and funny—presentation by Herman Kahn, then a major figure in Cold War circles. It had nothing to do with Viet Nam, but it was entertaining nonetheless.

Many of these newly recruited men were not only married, they also possessed families. This posed a problem, as all dependents of American military and civilian government personnel had been evacuated from Viet Nam in 1963, and no dependents were allowed to live "in country." New employees with families were given two choices: leave the family at home, get paid leave every six months and serve for an 18-month tour, or establish your dependents in one of several "safe haven" locations in countries nearby, visit more often and serve a two-year tour. My father chose the latter route. One of those safe havens was in the Philippines, and it was to Manila that we flew as a family via some time in Honolulu. This was my first trip overseas.

We moved into a large, beautiful home in a gated community called

San Lorenzo Village in Makati, a suburb of Manila. The house was leased by USAID, and we replaced a family that was about to return home. We inherited their two female live-in servants, so the transition was a smooth one. I immediately realized that we had just moved up quite a bit in status; we could never have afforded such a house in the U.S., let alone two servants! I found it a bit disconcerting when, during our welcome dinner hosted by the family moving out (the furniture remained, so this was easy), I watched our hostess summarily snap her fingers for a cigarette and saw Benita hasten to give her one and light it. These people had clearly enjoyed the privileges of rich Americans overseas a bit too much. We resolved to treat the servants better, and we did. In exchange, we learned how Filipina girls much preferred to work for Americans; their own elite treated them like dirt.

Makati was remarkably like an American suburb, albeit a very rich one. Automobiles proliferated but none of the (inevitably colorful) local trucks and "jeepneys" that passed by outside. Dad's contract allowed for the shipment of our car overseas, so we were soon established and functioning in a remarkably American environment. There was a supermarket that except for some differences in the food offered would have passed for an upscale American one just about anywhere. There was the International High School both my brothers would attend and graduate from. It was thus quite possible for a foreigner to live in Makati and have only passing encounters with the Filipinos. The U.S. Navy still had a considerable presence in Manila Bay, at Sangley Point and Subic Bay. Military dependents had been a continuous presence here for decades, which meant there were both a commissary and a PX, the former for food and the latter for just about anything else. As dependents of an American government employee, our family also had shopping privileges there, which involved a boat ride across a portion of Manila Bay, a trip that only made things more fun. The PX and commissary were priced for military family shoppers and offered bargains in just about everything. I would come to comprehend this remarkable condition more fully in Viet Nam.

This first visit also made obvious one of the most remarkable characteristics of urban life in what we called back then "the developing world": astonishing inequality within a remarkably close proximity. San Lorenzo Village would have qualified as an elite suburban community anywhere in the U.S. Add to that the climate, the flora, and deep pockets, and the result was that many of the homes in this development were even a cut above the high level of the rest—just gorgeous, landscaped and planted in an array of designs and colors, and almost all inhabited by Filipinos. There were other gated communities nearby that were even swankier than San Lorenzo Village and where no Americans had infiltrated, at least to live. It was here that I swam in my first—and last—indoor *and* outdoor residential swimming pool.

However, once you passed through the gate of such a village (always being saluted by the helmeted and uniformed guards), you were back in the real Philippines, a country groaning under the plundering hand of Ferdinand Marcos and his coterie. The roads were rather clear during the day, but by nightfall small fires dotted the road beginning immediately outside the gate, each tended by a small group of homeless, ill-clothed men and women. There was a shabby brothel about one hundred yards from the gated entrance. And that was just the beginning of the lesson. The international airport through which we had arrived would, a few years later, catch fire. The airport's ill-trained fire personnel quickly discovered that their hose lines were old and rotten, with most of the other equipment in similar shape, if it was present at all. The airport burned to the ground. It had cost a great deal of money to build, most of which went into the pockets of the politically connected contractors and much of that diverted to the politicians themselves. I would welcome the Laban revolution when it finally arrived and then weep when the potential drowned in corruption once again.

During my sophomore year at Georgetown, my father wrote me from Viet Nam to ask if I wanted to spend the coming summer of 1967 there, in Da Nang, where he was stationed. I agreed without hesitation. This was a rare opportunity, and I was determined to seize it. To actually go the place everybody was talking about so vehemently, to see for myself what so many people so passionately argued over with only decidedly second-hand (or less) knowledge was irresistible. I was already scheduled to fly to Manila, and Saigon wasn't much farther. Dad had arranged for me to work as a volunteer for the World Relief Commission (WRC), a Canada-based missionary organization (it exists today), then working through the international Christian and Missionary Alliance, an Evangelical organization of independent churches, primarily in the U.S. and Canada. As "missionary" is in its name, much of its focus lay outside North America, and Viet Nam was in great need of assistance. Dad told me that a retired husband

and wife were working for the WRC in Da Nang and I was going to assist them.

After my sophomore year concluded, I soon was again a passenger on Pan Am Flight 841, on my way to Manila. But this time, it would be only a quick stopover. I was going to Viet Nam.

Introduction

The Perspective of a Spear-Carrier

One morning in early June 1967 I was a very nervous passenger in a small, two-engine Air America plane flying from Saigon to Da Nang, in what was then the Republic of Viet Nam (South Viet Nam). We weren't flying very high, and the verdant and irregular landscape of central Viet Nam on our left and the blue of the South China Sea to our right made the scene deceptively beautiful. I had pretty much quieted my fear of flying in small planes when the pilot called back and asked us (he didn't need an intercom; it was a very small plane) to look on the ground below for the remains of "last week's flight." I immediately told myself he was joking (he was, it turned out), but the hook line from Larry Verne's surprise 1960 hit, "Please Mister Custer," started repeating itself in my mind: *What am I doing here?* We were, after all, flying over a modern "Indian Country," and I began to identify with his concern. Little did I know that I would have cause to repeat the phrase several times in the future—also in Viet Nam—but with different emphases.

The Viet Nam conflict was the central event of my adolescence and early adulthood. This was true, up to a point, for every young man of my generation because of the military draft, and I shared that common presence growing up, that shadow of doubt about what I would be doing after I graduated from college. But Viet Nam became much more for me, despite my being one of the lucky ones the draft did not touch. My experiences "in country" differ from the vast majority of other Americans who were there because I was a civilian. I spent a total of two years and two months "in country," encompassing two stays. I spent the summer of 1967 working as a volunteer for a protestant missionary organization. Upon graduation from college in 1969 I was offered a job with the U.S. Agency for International Development (USAID). After a year of language training, I returned to Viet Nam in mid–June 1970 and remained for two years. Contained within these pages are my memories of those periods.

The war in Viet Nam has amassed a considerable historiography. The vast majority of works focus either on the larger picture or on the personal stories of our military. Little has been written about "The Other War," generally referred to as "pacification." What does exist also focuses on the military. The role played by U.S. civilians in the effort to "win hearts and minds" is easily the aspect of the war most neglected in the historical record. What follows is a small contribution toward ending this neglect. This book is a memoir, not a researched work of history. It is an attempt to convey the atmosphere of the time and the place, the source of so many strange and improbable but true stories. I vividly remember several components of the "conventional wisdom," i.e., the manner in which we civilians spoke to each other, our jargon, and the things we believed to be true in such an environment: a war, but for us only sort of. I attempt to weave them into my text.

The most important thing to understand is that this tale is told from the perspective of a "spear-carrier." Upon my arrival in Saigon in 1970, I believed myself to be both the youngest and lowest-ranking member of the USAID staff in Viet Nam, an unofficial title I (may have) held for a year. It was that long before I met anyone both younger and lower ranking. I made no policy while there, but only executed the policies of others. My responsibilities advanced beyond what my pay grade normally would entail, but I was still just a figure lost in the crowd onstage, one expected to say nothing.

When you are a spear-carrier, you are on the big stage, in a big production, and very much aware of it. You are conscious of being part of something important, but exactly what is unclear from your perspective. That's because, for a spear-carrier, the view sucks. You obtain an intimate understanding of the details of your immediate surroundings, but even a glimpse of anything broader is pure chance. You get an excellent idea of how things are going in your immediate vicinity, and this occupies your full attention. You do get glimpses of the larger issue, but only if you can divert enough of your attention from your personal situation to catch them when they are visible. Whether you are on the winning or losing side often has to be explained to you later, as it isn't obvious from where you are.

Introduction

As I hope will be evident, my Viet Nam journey was like many others in that I went from blind acceptance of the war to knowledgeable opposition. How unlike so many others my journey turned out to be will unfold in the following pages. Viet Nam was a transformative experience, and it has left me with an abiding dislike of (in alphabetical order) anyone who says "love it or leave it," armchair patriots, fanatics of any persuasion, flag wavers, and those individuals for whom the highest goal is to be a "team player," to name but a few. The following pages explain why.

Some Personal Notes on Sensitive Subjects

The events that begin this book happened over 50 years ago. I thus have had to confront the limitations and weaknesses of my memory. I retain memories largely as visual images, although the facial and background details fade over time. While I took special effort to retain some memories, I never attempted to write down dates, much less remember them. That will be obvious in what follows. I have always had a problem remembering someone's name, even in the short run. The American names in the text that follow, save those well known to history, are all pseudonyms except for John and Carolyn Miller, who are mentioned in Chapter One, and Colonel Lawrence Thompson, the provincial senior advisor of Advisory Team #38 in Bao Loc. I have retained no connections with anyone, and as I had no way of contacting them I could not secure necessary permissions. I deeply regret this. These people deserve to be remembered, but the law is the law. I will refer to the Vietnamese by the names by which I knew them, because that is actually only their first name. Thus my primary contact at the Ministry of Social Welfare will be referred to as "Major Ba." This was the equivalent of my being addressed as "Mr. Mike," but it is how the Vietnamese structure their names.

I spent a year learning the Vietnamese language, and will attempt to describe the relationship between a tonal language and English, as there is much to learn about our follies in Viet Nam from this one vantage point. The Vietnamese language can be difficult to render in written English, for reasons I partly explain in Chapter Two. This can lead to misunderstandings and more.

I utilize in my writing two acronyms that do not meet academic muster: VC and NVA. The first stands for *Cong San Viet Nam*: "Vietnamese Communist," shortened to "Viet Cong," then "VC." The Government of the Republic of [South] Viet Nam (GVN) originated the term in the 1950s to describe its enemy in political terms. The Americans came to apply VC to those who were indigenous to the South, to differentiate them from the northerners, whom they referred to as the NVA, or North Vietnamese Army. The proper term is Peoples' Army of Viet Nam, or PAVN. I employ both of these politically incorrect terms in the text because this is a memoir, not a researched work, and those were the terms we used at the time. The occasions in which I employ them are significant. I use Viet Cong and VC in the chapter on my first visit to Viet Nam and for anecdotes that employ the word. Upon my return in 1970, I use NVA almost exclusively. This reflects the fundamental change in both the nature of the war and the enemy itself that occurred after Tet of 1968. My summer visit was in 1967, when the VC were the GVN's primary antagonist. Tet of '68 was a disaster for the indigenous Viet Cong cadres of South Viet Nam. They were slaughtered in city after city and never regained either their numerical strength or their battlefield prominence. The remnants remained active, but in the months and years after Tet 1968 the NVA steadily increased both its presence and its activity in the South. I arrived during the latter part of this transition period and was still in country when the first demonstration of this change—the Easter Offensive—took place.

Finally, in one small but consistent act of defiance, throughout the text I refer to my host country as Viet Nam. Almost no one writes it this way in English, but I spent a year immersed in its language, culture and history, then lived two years there, and that's how it should be rendered. Vietnamese is a monosyllabic language. I think we really ought to do better. We Americans altered several names, including *Sai Gon*, but I do not take this to excess, as being a perfectionist in this regard would only result in confusion. Therefore I use the more common forms for all other names.

ONE

What I Did on My Summer Vacation

June–August 1967

Upon arrival in the Philippines, I stayed with my mother for about a week at her house in Makati. She was not too pleased about my upcoming summer in Viet Nam but knew better than to make a point of it. Then it was on to Saigon—on a tourist visa. My status as a government dependent had paid my airfare from Washington, D.C., to Manila. My family had only to pay for what was a short flight to Saigon and back. I packed lightly, as I would be spending only a short time in a hot climate. Having lived the previous summer in Manila, I thought I was used to Southeast Asia's climate. I was wrong—very, very wrong. As I climbed down the ramp from the plane to the tarmac (no moving walkways back then) at Tan Son Nhut Airport, Saigon, the heat hit me with almost physical force, like I was descending into a blast furnace. The old terminal building was hugely overcrowded, which certainly didn't help.

I was sure there were shuttle buses between the airport and downtown (I would ride a few during my next visit), but as I was officially a tourist traveling alone, I simply hailed one of the local taxis, an old—and quite small—Renault painted in cream and blue. Even getting in was difficult; there could not possibly have been a second passenger. My destination was the Rex Hotel, an older building taken over by MACV and used as a temporary Bachelor Officer's Quarters (BOQ). Upon arrival, I paid what I was sure was an exorbitant amount for the trip, and the driver tried very hard to get me to pay in U.S. dollars, or something called "scrip." I had procured only Vietnamese piasters, which he grudgingly accepted. I didn't know it, but this was my introduction to one of the fundamental problems for which the U.S. presence was responsible. I would learn more.

A Spear-Carrier in Viet Nam

Entering the Rex Hotel required passing through a tall, sandbagged bunker and making a turn before entering the building proper. I was told that the bunker and its L shape were designed to protect the hotel not just from gunfire but also a bomb thrown from a vehicle. I was in a war zone now.

Protection from bombs existed, but noise was a different matter entirely. Each of the rooms had an air conditioner installed and the hum from it in the small room was quite noticeable. Loud though the AC was, it was overshadowed by the noise from the streets outside. The Rex Hotel sat in a prominent corner of downtown Saigon adjacent to a traffic circle, and the high-pitched whine of two-stroke engines filled the air, accompanied by the lower notes of various four-stroke models. When night came and I went to bed I discovered that Saigon is also a city that never sleeps. The traffic noise barely abated, even in the middle of the night, and that air conditioner seemed even louder. I got little sleep, and at one point actually turned on a light and began to read, hoping for the best. If I had known what my second night in Viet Nam would be like, I would have tried harder to get some sleep.

My summer in the Philippines had also given me the impression that vehicle traffic in and around that capital city was the most diverse and disorganized such traffic could possibly be. It took only a ride from Tan Son Nhut to Saigon on one day and a return trip the next, plus a few down hours downtown spent watching the traffic, to convince me that I had been very wrong about that too. Saigon's "atmosphere" can be described in three words: heat, noise, and smoke. The heat lay over everything, and both the noise and the smoke—at least most of it—had the same source: small Japanese motorcycles, the 50cc–90cc types. They were everywhere, all the time, operating by a very casual driver's code, little impeded by traffic lights and not at all by the local police. Manila had nowhere near their number.

When it came to diversity, Saigon won hands down, although Manila was far more colorful. Saigon had nothing like the garishly decorated "Jeepneys" that served as Manila's primary form of public transport, but it had everything from bicycles (many of them) to large army 2½-ton ("deuce and a half") trucks, with many odd machines in between, some of which I have never seen elsewhere. Going strictly by numbers, I would guess that there were more pedal vehicles than motor vehicles on the road. The vast majority of these were bicycles, but Saigon still possessed a number of pedicabs known as cyclos, a long-time standard in Asian cities. The Vietnamese variety was a three-wheeled vehicle with a seat for a single passenger up front, between two wheels. The operator sat up high and behind, pedaling a single rear wheel. Steering was accomplished by the operator turning the front portion of the frame, which included the seat and its passenger along with the front wheels. There was also a movable shade over the passenger seat to protect against either sun or rain, at least to some extent. The driver was protected only by his pith helmet. Cyclos were a relic of another time, slower and more tranquil, before the advent of the internal combustion engine. Saigon was a city full of people going somewhere as fast as they possibly could, in a wide variety of vehicles. The sedate pace of a cyclo was a glaring anachronism. Slow and romantic, it would have been more romantic had it been able to accommodate more than one person.

There was a form of cyclo that could do just that, one of the strangest vehicles I have ever seen and one I have neither seen nor heard of anywhere else. This was the "motorized cyclo," and its resemblance to the smaller pedal version was obvious. The layout was the same, but it had a front seat wide enough for two people (or sometimes more). There was no sunshade over the passenger/s, but the driver sat up and to the rear as with the original version. Below him was a single-cylinder gasoline engine of indeterminate make and vintage that did the work of pushing this much-heavier contraption around. A motorized cyclo was not that fast, but when you are sitting a few inches above the asphalt in the very front of something weaving in and out of Saigon traffic you are going more than fast enough. The passengers sat over the front axle, and a steel pipe was both the front bumper and the passengers' footrest. This meant that the forward-most parts of this vehicle were your toes. Not to mention the fact that, if your driver hit anything you would be catapulted headfirst into whatever it was. The driver actually steered the small front wheels on this model, which made tight turns much too possible. As frightening as the ride was, the riders were quite happy that they were in the front, because that meant the engine was behind them. The noise of the engine was the usual annoying, high-pitched two-stroke sound, and having it behind you really helped. By far more important was that the smoke it produced so copiously was also behind you. Every motorized cyclo I ever saw (and I only ever saw them in Saigon) smoked like it was powered by coal. Each one would lay a continuous belt of smoke behind it to the point of obscuring things for the other vehicles, bicycles in particular.

Mind you, while the motorized cyclos were the greatest offenders, the operative word for Saigon traffic was "smoke" (closely followed by "chaos"), and motorized cyclos were not numerous enough to contribute more than a small part to the constantly present white, roiling cloud produced by a multitude of improperly tuned engines. Motorized cyclos at least had the excuse of being old, while the huge number of small Japanese motorcycles incessantly buzzing about Saigon were quite new. New or not, they virtually all smoked; the only difference was one of degree. The motorized cyclo was a design that can most generously be described as "dangerous," but the real danger was Saigon traffic itself. This danger was partially due to the large variety of vehicles on the streets, all interweaving with the rest of the traffic. It was mostly due, however, to the almost complete lack of traffic control. Stoplights and even traffic cops existed, but they were ignored if people thought they could get away with whatever it was they were doing—and in Saigon during this time people could get away with just about anything. Traffic ostensibly drove on the right, but a row of shady trees over a street could seriously affect that. I quickly surmised that the only real law governing traffic was the law of the jungle; you drove roughshod over anything smaller than you and meekly gave way to anything bigger than you. My first visit was just for overnight, and I got only a taste of the variegated madhouse that was Saigon traffic. I would learn much more on my second visit, when I lived in Saigon and drove every day.

Although my time in Saigon was quite brief on this initial visit, I saw for the first time something that I would see many times again, but only in Saigon. A motorized cyclo had broken down while it was going around a downtown traffic circle. Its driver had begun to fix it exactly where it had stopped, right in the middle of traffic. He had the cylinder head off and various tools nearby as the traffic of all sorts calmly went around him *on both sides*. He hadn't moved his vehicle one inch from where it had come to a stop. Much later, as I observed this phenomenon over and over again, I would see it as a metaphor for the people of South Viet Nam.

I did get a shuttle to the airport this time, from the Rex Hotel, and was dropped off at the Air America terminal. By "terminal" I mean a hut of corrugated metal whose open doors and windows and internal fans did little to relieve the oppressive heat such buildings create inside. My father had booked me on a flight to Da Nang. This would be my introduction to an airline that was little known in the rest of the world but was the very lifeline of Americans in South Viet Nam: CIA-operated "Air America."

Postwar attention has focused on Air America's role in the hidden but nearby conflicts in Laos and Cambodia, and rightly so. Yet to most of us in Viet Nam, it was Air America that got us to wherever it was we wanted to go. It provided regularly scheduled flights to and from all province capitals from the regional centers, and flights out of Saigon to those centers. It also provided, as I would soon learn, charter services to haul commodities, pretty much regardless of destination. The scheduled flight to Da Nang was my first experience aboard Air America, but it would quickly be followed by others.

There were several flights listed (on a chalkboard) going to several places, so the terminal was actually rather active, considering that most everyone there was consciously trying to move as little as possible unless it meant getting closer to one of the fans. My first Air America flight—which appears in the introduction to this book—was on a Volpar, one of the many types of planes that Americans would rightly consider to be obscure if not unknown, which constituted the Air America fleet. Although it looked rather modern, a Volpar was a design as old its larger Air America brethren, the C-46 and C-47. It had originated as a Beechcraft Model 18 back to the 1930s. Volpar had modernized the old design, which included removing the Beech's radial engines and replacing them with turboprops. This shifted the plane's weight forward enough to require a tricycle landing gear. The original Beech had been a "tail dragger" layout. By Air America standards, flying in a Volpar was traveling first class: it possessed recognizable seats. Nothing else I ever flew in came even close. While I was in Dalat somewhat later, I saw the one used by U.S. ambassador to South Viet Nam, Ellsworth Bunker, as his personal in-country transportation, thus confirming its status.

That Second Night

My Saigon to Da Nang shuttle flight with the pilot and his macabre sense of humor passed without incident (we never saw any crash remains) and I was deposited at the quite large U.S. airbase just outside the city. Air America also had a terminal there. It was a small, nondescript metal shack only somewhat larger than many other equally nondescript shacks strewn around the countryside that I would encounter. The airbase itself was another matter—huge, and the home of several units of military planes. Da Nang was Viet Nam's second largest city. The city itself was located at the mouth of the Da Nang River, which made it a seaport for small cargo ships, trawlers and the like. The old town center featured wide boulevards, shaded streets, typical tall French buildings with equally tall windows, and some rather sumptuous residences, all on a rather small and limited scale. The more utilitarian ones had been taken over by various U.S. agencies, and the U.S. presence was ubiquitous.

Da Nang city was surrounded—and dwarfed—by rings of U.S. military installations intermixed with ugly little communities of Vietnamese, mostly refugees living a hand-to-mouth existence in the scrappiest of buildings, cobbled together from corrugated roofing sheets and the remains of old soda cans. The airbase itself was quite substantial, the home of tactical, fighter, and observation units. It had an airstrip long enough to take even commercial jets. It had not been long enough, however, for a B-52 that had attempted an emergency landing sometime earlier, with tangibly bad results that remained just off the end of the runway. The sprawling III Marine Amphibious Force (MAF) compound lay nearby. South of town was the R&R center known as "China Beach." We even had a battery of Hawk antiaircraft missiles stationed in the high pass among the hills north of town.

After exiting the airbase, I simply hailed a cyclo and told him *Tin Lanh*, ("Protestant" in Vietnamese). It was enough, even in my mutilated pronunciation. In a largely Buddhist country with a substantial Catholic minority, Protestants were few and far between, having just a few locations here and there. These would mostly be in the highlands, as I would soon discover, but there was one in Da Nang, and to it I was taken. My cyclo driver had no trouble getting me to the compound, and I got my first up-close view of Viet Nam outside Saigon. Da Nang traffic was a much smaller version of that in the capital, much less congested (and way less smoky), and with an even larger portion of bicycles. I saw a few of the same vintage Renault taxis and even fewer of the even more vintage Citroen sedans that transported the most important Vietnamese civilians, but no motorized cyclos.

No one was at the compound to greet me, but I had been told not to expect anyone. My hosts, Mr. and Mrs. Warren, were away but expected back the next day, and my father was also away. Despite a lack of guidance, I had no trouble finding my way around the surprisingly substantial compound. It contained the Warren's modest house, some smaller buildings (ostensibly classrooms, as I was later informed) and a larger building, all constructed in the French style, with high ceilings and large windows. The larger building (which apparently had housed different operations at different times) was where I would sleep. Or so I thought. I took a quick walk around the building in the fading light and noticed that some pieces of the masonry, mostly near windows and doors, had been torn away, evidently quite roughly. Could it have been from gunfire, I wondered? I later learned I was right, but no one could remember by whom or when, including the Warrens, who had lived in the compound for almost a year.

My room in the larger building was itself large, but with only a chair, a suitably small desk and a narrow bed against one wall. The bed had been made, with a mattress—a thin one, but I didn't care much about that sort of thing back then—and two sheets, plus a slim pillow and its pillowcase. The windows were tall and open, and a ceiling fan spun slowly above. Neither of these last did anything to lessen the wet, stifling heat that lay over everything, everywhere. I undressed, showered, and lay down on the bed.

Mr. and Mrs. Warren, with recently arrived supplies, at the Tin Lanh compound, summer 1967.

A Spear-Carrier in Viet Nam

Even as I first lay down, I could feel the rivulets of sweat collecting and rolling down by body, my face, everywhere. I had been sweating since I got off the plane, relieved briefly by my shower, but this was the worst. If I simply lay in bed doing nothing but breathing, I could feel the sweat bead and roll down all over my body. Movement of any sort only increased the volume of sweat.

What followed was the most uncomfortable night of my life, its total wretchedness never equaled through all the nights in subsequent decades. The atmosphere was beyond stifling; I was trapped inside what seemed like a steam bath. I could not sleep. I turned the ceiling fan up to high and uneasily eyed it as it swung from its mount, the long pole swaying alarmingly in a steady circular motion. But there was no noticeable improvement in my condition. I have always needed some sort of cover when sleeping, a purely psychological thing, I think. As the top sheet blocked what little effect the fan had on the air below, it slowly got wet and adhered to more and more of my body. I began to reconsider my sheet policy and soon stripped it off and laid back down. Again, no difference. After a short time I moved the bed to the middle of the room, directly under the fan, my fears about its uncertain mounting be damned. Nothing improved, and I continued to lie there, sweating, feeling rivulet after rivulet form on my body, then drip down, everywhere.

I probably fell asleep at some point, although my dreams were of heat and sweat, if they were dreams at all. In the morning, I got up off the bed and noticed that my sheet was one large sweat stain, darkest in the general shape of my body down the middle, that had spread out almost to the corners of the sheet itself. My pillowcase was not just damp, it was sodden. I stripped it off and actually wrung out sweat from it by twisting it. My pillow was also soaking wet virtually all over, as I had moved my head to different positions on it during the night, vainly seeking some relief.

After a shower—one of the finest I can remember, although the water was tepid and came out of the nozzle only fitfully—I did a quick rub-off with a thoroughly inadequate towel that dried my body for a brief time before I began to sweat again. I began to consider how I was going to survive the coming weeks. Then my salvation arrived—in the form of my father. He lived not far away in the CORDS civilian compound.[1] This was an example of the pre-fab and floorplan-adjustable compounds I would become quite familiar with on my return visit. There was an unoccupied AIR-CONDITIONED bedroom in one of the units, and my father had obtained permission (from whom was never specified) for me to occupy it. I wasted no time at all accepting the offer and moved in that day. It made all the difference. I honestly don't know how I could have functioned while living out of that sweatbox I had spent my first night in.

Mr. Warren and his wife also returned later that day, and as I ate dinner with them they outlined their mission and discussed how I could contribute. They worked for the World Relief Commission (WRC), itself a component of the Christian and Missionary Alliance (C&MA), which operated the compound. The WRC was (and remains) a Canada-based missionary organization. The Warrens had attempted to operate an animal husbandry school in some of the buildings but confessed that it had been a failure and was currently inactive. They showed me a public relations photo and text about a young Vietnamese man who had, through the program, become an "expert chicken farmer." None of it was true, Mr. Warren said; the kid was worthless, lazy, and a thief. The primary function of the WRC in Viet Nam thus became to distribute commodities and clothes donated by the members of C&MA congregations in the United States and Canada. The items that had arrived were being kept in warehouse space in the Da Nang airport complex that had been loaned to the WRC. The work of processing these bags had fallen behind and would become the first part of my job. I was to sort through the bags and collect the useful items. Then I was to accompany the shipments of these commodities to ensure that they reached the intended recipients at each location. The flights would be Air America charters. Air America would not ship unaccompanied merchandise, so someone (other than a Vietnamese) had to go with each flight. That would be me.

There was a Tin Lanh church of some size (and more colorful decorations than are customary in American/Canadian churches) in Da Nang, and the C&MA/WRC compound was located in the city also because it was a populous enough location and accessible by sea as well as air. The center of Tin Lanh activity in Viet Nam, however, was in the central highlands, and the center of that was in Dalat. The Protestants didn't have anywhere near the missionary staff the Catholics had, and operated in a much more independent fashion.

My father couldn't wait to show me around Da Nang. His office was at the regional headquarters, another complex of older buildings altered into some semblance of a fortification. There was B-40 wire wrapped around the perimeter and bunkers inside it. Civilians—and a number of military—ate at the mess hall/projection room, a large building known as "the White Elephant." It combined regular meals with occasional movies. The ambient din from the former greatly interfered with enjoyment of the latter.

The food was good and substantial (meaning high caloric), but it was the milk my father raved about. "You have to taste the milk," he said. "It's the best you ever drank." I tried some, and he was right, it was—rich and creamy and absolutely the tastiest ever. "It's reconstituted, of course," he continued. "It comes over as powder." The secret, he said, was peanut oil added to the powder and water mix. I was never able to confirm that, but damn, that was good milk, indeed the best I ever drank.

I did not return to Da Nang during my second visit, so I never found out if the milk was still as sweet and good, and I never encountered it anywhere else. I didn't miss the milk that much; I had all but stopped drinking it before going to Viet Nam in 1967. I didn't miss the milk, but boy did I miss the chocolate. Chocolate as we know it could not exist in that climate due to the heat and the almost complete lack of refrigeration. The solution to the dilemma this posed for me—I am an unrepentant chocoholic—was sold in Viet Nam as "Hershey's Tropical Chocolate," which was at least truth in advertising, because it would have sold nowhere else. It was just god-awful. Imagine if you can, what you know as chocolate with all, repeat ALL the moisture removed. It came in a bar, rather small actually, that chewing slowly reduced to a desert-dry powder. It also had the barest chocolate taste. If you consciously summoned up some extra saliva and used your tongue to work it into the powder, a hint of chocolate might waft across a few taste buds. It wasn't worth the effort to eat, although I suspected it was chock-full of calories for jungle sustenance.

The CORDS residence compound in Da Nang was where I spent my nights, but little time otherwise. I was not part of the team and didn't want to press the point. The compound was where I first encountered what was a ritual at U.S. civilian locations throughout the country. As I drove up to the front gate—which was always kept closed—two men would come to my vehicle, each carrying what looked like an oversize dustpan with a long vertical handle. The "pan" at the bottom was actually a mirror, set at an angle so that its holder could peer up into the underside of the vehicle chassis. Both men would slowly walk down the length of my car, looking for bombs that might have been attached there. Finding none, they would signal the gate, which would open. The mirror men were local civilians, but the compound had its own set of guards. They were Nungs, an ethnic minority that, by consensus, produced the hardest fighting and most reliable of the Vietnamese.

My father was clearly enjoying his time here on the frontier. In his off hours, he had become friends with a remarkably wide array of people, few of whom could be called educated, let alone intellectual. I did spend a good amount of time with one such group, three navy servicemen, all of them longtime enlisted men who served as instructors at the Da Nang Tech School. The school had been built just before my father's time there, but he was involved in its administration. The three men taught auto mechanics and driver's education during the day and had somehow contrived to set themselves up to live in a corner of the tech school itself, on the second floor, all of it surrounded with B-40 wire. They had established quite a comfortable nest, with most of the comforts of home, at least as related to alcohol. I quite enjoyed just sitting around as the three old hands got drunk (which they did, quite religiously, every night) and told stories.

One night while I was present they decided to implement a plan they had been hatching, to steal a water buffalo. In this context, understand that "water buffalo" was slang for a potable water tank mounted on a two-wheel trailer. I, with typical lack of thoughtful consideration, asked to go with them. They agreed, and we drove out into the night in our navy Bronco and onto a military base. I believe it was a navy site but wasn't sure then and didn't ask later. They had previously located their target and found it easily. We backed up to it and hooked it onto the vehicle's military-style hitch. We then drove off and somehow got waved out through the gate, to safety. I say "somehow" because we were in a Ford Bronco, which had not been designed to tow a water buffalo. The tank was something close to full, and its tongue weight caused the vehicle's rear to squat down, flattening the rear springs and almost bursting the tires, while pointing the vehicle's hood up in the air. The sentry that waved us through had to be paying no attention whatsoever. We returned with the "requisitioned" water buffalo, and they added it to their collection of items with which they lived pretty well in the middle of a war.

A fundamental part of the particular slang that every war situation adopts was, in Viet Nam, a ranking system to indicate pleasure or displeasure with what one had just heard or been told about. It was numeric, but only sort of, and had only two components. The first was "Number One!," which was an expression of absolute approval and the other was

"Number Ten!," which expressed the polar opposite. There were no gradations in this system; things were either "Number One" or "Number Ten," despite everyone's unspoken knowledge that things were not nearly that simple. I was distressed to learn shortly after arriving in Da Nang in 1967 to hear my father, the EdD, use the expression with me frequently.

Not far away from Da Nang was a hill somewhat grandly called Marble Mountain. It was no mountain, and what it produced may not actually have been marble. My father presented me with a triangular piece from there, several inches long, with my name and "Da Nang, Vietnam, 1967" carved into it. It makes one hell of a paperweight. I heard later that several "marble mountains" exist near some of the major cities along the coast, also doing a lucrative trade to the Americans. My father was also the first to tell me of the unfortunate symbolism offered by the flag of the Republic of Viet Nam. Driving me downtown shortly after I arrived, he pointed at the flag waving over a nearby building and remarked, "See that flag? It tells you all you need to know. All that's not red is yellow." I, within a few years, would conclude that while the phrase may not have been entirely true, it pretty much summed up the situation.

Mr. Warren drove me onto the Da Nang airbase and showed me how to get to the warehouse that held the WRC material. The Warrens drove a station wagon, a Frontenac, a Canadian Ford. They had little use for it, so it became my vehicle, taking me from the CORDS compound where I lived to the Tin Lanh compound and the warehouse. This put me in one of the larger vehicles on the Da Nang streets, but I didn't take that seriously. I was the foreigner and had no desire to lord it over the bicyclists and motorcyclists that composed most of the city's traffic. My ability to drive about the town without getting into accidents was apparently unusual, and it was commented on.

The warehouse on the airbase was the standard metal-framed and metal-sheathed, low-pitched roof type seen so often in the States. The WRC material was piled in one corner, in what had become something of a hill up to the highest point of the pile in the corner. I began to work, initially just in the most general manner of trying to understand what I was dealing with and how to organize it. The process required several days, and indeed was never finished. Uncounted numbers of clothing items had been collected by individual C&MA churches, collected into coarse burlap bags and somehow directed to this one warehouse in Viet Nam. This had been going on for some time evidently, with the bags just being piled up and left. The job became no fun at all in no time at all. That metal-roofed warehouse was sitting in the Da Nang sun, and the inside of it was an absolute oven. The total lack of air movement didn't help, particularly because every step I took kicked up dust and burlap fibers. The air over the pile would become choked with this toxic mess, and I needed to go outside periodically. This brought an improvement in my breathing, but being outside in the sun was no fun. Had this effort brought forth something positive, I would have noticed the discomfort a great deal less. Unfortunately, I quickly discovered that the overwhelming amount of the items I was sorting through were of absolutely no use in Viet Nam. Each item had been donated through an organized church activity, bagged, collected from a multitude of separate sources, and shipped across at least part of the North American continent and then the Pacific Ocean, all to end up here in one large pile in a baking-hot warehouse. Through all of this effort it does not seem to have occurred to anyone to think about just what items might be useful in such a climate or to people in these circumstances.

I estimated that shoes constituted at least three-quarters of the total, with women's shoes outnumbering men's by a huge amount. They varied greatly in state of wear and overall condition, but that really didn't matter, as 95 percent of them were high heels, which also didn't matter because virtually every pair was too large for a Vietnamese woman's foot. The far fewer men's shoes demonstrated the same size problem, only worse. Those good Christians who had donated items of clothing had pretty much fallen into the same trap as far as size, and no one appears to have told them that heavy coats, woolen hats, and snow boots were not appropriate for the destination.

Several hot, sweaty and dust-filled days in the WRC warehouse produced a distressingly small pile of items that were actually useful. Mr. Warren called a halt to the work. We collected a few of what he thought would be the most useful items, and I was surprised to see that light sweaters and shawls were among them. The climate was different in the Central Highlands he said, and such light wraps were needed in the early mornings and late evenings. Mr. Warren told me that I was going to see this for myself, as the WRC had recently received a substantial shipment of medical supplies. He had decided to add the useful items from the warehouse to this shipment and send them all to the headquarters of WRC activity, the city of Dalat in the Central Highlands. Both he and I were to accompany the flight, and his company served to introduce me to the protocol and procedures involved in civilians flying around a war zone.

That's when I began to understand that however difficult Protestant Christian proselyting among the Vietnamese was in a Buddhist country largely ruled by Catholics, the people of the Central Highlands, the Montagnards, were a great deal more receptive. These people, racially and culturally distinct from Vietnamese and both tribally and linguistically fragmented among themselves, had remained largely isolated from the development of Vietnamese civilization. They were something out of *National Geographic*, with bare-breasted women in colorful robes and dark-skinned men wielding stone axes. By this time, of course, they had been rudely introduced to Western civilization, and thus had both metal tools and weapons. The Montagnards were confined to the highlands, and the tribes in Viet Nam constituted but a few of the multitude of tribes and peoples that inhabit the vast highlands of Southeast Asia. The Montagnards being oppressed by the Vietnamese, Protestant missionaries thus found them much more receptive to the Protestant version of the word of God than were their overlords.

The trip to Dalat was my first flight out of Da Nang, my first delivery of items, and the first time I ever laid eyes on a C-46, let alone flown in one. The C-46 looked for all the world like a C-47 in the last stages of pregnancy. It had a bulbous belly, and everything about it just seemed like a C-47 that had gained weight. Its width, wings, engines, landing gear, nose, and tail were all like a C-47's but slightly larger and more swollen. This one had no seats of any sort, so Mr. Warren and I had to make ourselves comfortable amidst the cargo. This turned out to be a useful introduction to travel by air in Viet Nam. The flight was uneventful, and I spent my time looking at the remarkable scenery of the Central Highlands, which was rugged and verdant. There was also much evidence of war. We frequently flew over what were obviously bomb craters of substantial size, circular areas where the vegetation had been blasted into oblivion. I did notice one or two areas that were significantly different, however. They were large, remarkably symmetrical rectangles of ground (I couldn't begin to estimate how large) that were totally free of any ground cover. Their brownness contrasted hugely with the areas all around them. I filed away the questions that this odd sight raised for another time.

We landed in Dalat, the biggest and most-developed town in the Central Highlands, although that wasn't saying much. Dalat had been a vacation retreat for the French and Emperor Bao Dai and was the economic center for the many plantations scattered around it. The first thing to strike me after we had landed, taxied over to an unloading area, and opened the rear door was the temperature. It was warm but by no means hot, and it was utterly lacking in the humidity that accompanies the heat on the coastal lowlands. Mr. Warren had been right, and I quickly fell in love with the area. It was just beautiful. He and I stayed only that night, but this brief introduction to a very different climate not all that far away began my instruction in just how varied Viet Nam was, and this in just the southern half.

That one night in Dalat was a memorable one. Mr. Warren's arrival together with the shipment of medical supplies seemed to stimulate a gathering of Protestant missionaries from around the Central Highlands. We all (ten or so) gathered for dinner, then sat around in a large room while everyone reminisced about their work in Viet Nam and of those who had come before them. It was a magical evening—of fellowship rooted in faith among people who were living and working that faith. I heard stories about tiger hunting and travelling on Bao Dai's elephants, and many about the eccentricities of some of the missionaries, human beings all. The Tin Lanh contingent had been in country for decades, and had accumulated a wealth of tales. I just sat in a corner, said nothing, and listened to people you hear little about discuss an entirely different Viet Nam than one everyone read about. Many years later, the summer of 1967 would find its place in American lore as "the summer of love." My memory of that summer is rather short on love—there wasn't much of that going around—but for that one night, and that one night only, love was in the air, and it was the love of God.

That first Dalat trip was also the only time I returned via a scheduled flight with my name on the manifest. We flew on a II Corps shuttle to Nha Trang, then to Da Nang. Every other flight out of Da Nang during my two months in country was chartered in advance with Air America, but one-way only. All but two of my deliveries would be to highland areas, some in I Corps but also in II Corps to the south. Together they demonstrated that the security situation in Viet Nam was nowhere near as good as the charts one saw on TV would seem to claim. The difference was night and day, quite literally. Our Vietnamese roamed freely during the day (although they tended to roam where there was less chance of encountering the enemy), but by nightfall every organization we had armed to resist the VC would button themselves up in their defended

27

compounds, surrendering the night to the opposition. Civilians—even American ones—could utilize the roads for trips provided you could reach a populated area—or return to your point of origin—between sunrise and sunset. That also applied to the many volunteer organizations in country and thus to me.

I made almost all of my deliveries by plane and only one delivery from the WRC warehouse by road. This was a trip to take food supplies to a Tin Lanh church in Quang Ngai. The pastor insisted I remain for "the ceremony of receiving the supplies." The truck driver had been instructed to obey me, so we stayed. This not-too-brief moment served as my introduction to the Vietnamese custom of holding a public ceremony for just about every step of every project. I would learn more about this later. Every load of commodities had to have an American escort, and for the WRC that was me. I usually flew in C-47s. I had never flown in one before this, but I was familiar with the C-47, which had made ubiquitous appearances in my reading about World War II. They had been the supply workhorses in that war and were resurrected for the same role in Viet Nam. They were by far the most common type of plane I would encounter, both that summer and on my return.

Me aboard a truckload of supplies bound for Dalat, summer 1967.

28

C-47s (and C-46s, for that matter) were flown by a team of pilot and copilot. All loading and unloading was ultimately my responsibility. The plane would invariably leave immediately after disgorging my commodities and me. Those at my destination had usually been informed in advance of my arrival (at least the day if not quite the exact time), and no one wanted to leave any commodities out in the open for very long, escorted or not, so I never had any trouble getting my items to their intended destination. Getting back to Da Nang, however, was a lot more problematic and entirely up to chance. Wherever I was in I Corps, I knew that most flights were going to Da Nang sooner or later. The Marines also operated a large base at Phu Bai, and I passed through it more than once. My trips down to the Central Highlands were dicier because of the lack of inter-regional flights, and they were also fewer in number. Catching a ride home usually meant hanging around the local airstrip, waiting as each plane or helicopter arrived, and then asking the loadmaster or whoever got off of each craft two questions: "Where are you going?" and "Can I hitch a ride?" The novelty of having a young American civilian ask for a lift never seemed to wear off, and I was rarely refused. I could, however, be bumped at a stop along the way if necessary to meet weight limits, and I was twice, once for a pallet of toilet paper. There are priorities, after all.

I made one return trip on another of the many World War II-vintage airplanes that were everyday sights in Viet Nam, a C-123. This was a twin-engine, high-wing cargo plane that had evolved from a World War II glider design, or so I was told. Those suckers could both get down and get up very quickly. The hydraulic tailgate, together with the rollers in the storage deck, also facilitated quick unloading, as was dramatically revealed to me. My ride on one—it was a U.S. Army aircraft—would eventually take me to Da Nang, but first it was to make a drop-off at an obscure district headquarters town I never learned the name of, or rather the barely-there dirt airstrip that serviced it. The loadmaster in the back with me mentioned that the pilots were going to overfly the site and look for a flare. Green meant "come on down," while a red one meant "under attack, come back later." Green it was, and we suddenly made a steep descent and briefly seemed to be landing on a small river before alighting on the dirt airstrip that began just across it. Engines roared as the pilots reversed props, and we quickly came to the end of the short airstrip. The plane turned around, and as the tailgate lowered, the loadmaster unhooked the straps holding the pallets to the rollers built into the floor. With the tailgate just above ground level, a burst of throttle sent the pallets cascading to the rear, off the plane and onto the ground. This offload was actually the first phase of the takeoff, as the tailgate began to rise and the plane to gather speed. We barely cleared the runway at the bank of the river on takeoff—very quick, very efficient, and very telling about the state of security in that location.

My initial encounter with Air America had been the Volpar flight from Saigon to Da Nang and the pilot with the wry sense of humor. It wasn't a good beginning, but my opinion of Air America swung around to the opposite extreme quite quickly. I have always been afraid of heights, and several decades after Viet Nam I was formally diagnosed with something the doctor calls "benign situational vertigo." I was uncomfortable flying on large jets and had no idea what my work in Viet Nam might be, but my confrontation with flying around in a variety of antique aircraft came quickly. To my total surprise, I quickly grew comfortable with flying Air America, inspired entirely by their pilots, real seat-of-the-pants guys.

A scare shortly into my time there actually cemented this feeling. I was in a C-47 headed to Kontum, in northern II Corps, from Da Nang. We were flying over some hilly jungle when the right engine quit. I was startled, but assured myself that the plane had been designed to fly on one engine. Then the left engine quit. The whistling of the wind outside suddenly became deafening. I jumped up from the provisional seat I had built by arranging boxes and bags, and walked to just outside the cabin in something close to panic mode. The pilots seemed remarkably unconcerned. The copilot flipped a switch, looked, and swore: "Damn gook mechanics! They forgot to fill the damn tank!" He then flipped the switch for another tank, which fortunately turned out to have gas in it. First the right engine cranked, coughed, and caught, and then the left one. I began to breathe again, but it was quite a while before my heart returned to something approximating its normal rate. Both pilots were quite nonchalant about the whole thing, as apparently things like this happened and were just part of the job.

It was this air of quiet competence, visible to all (unlike in a commercial jet where one has no idea what is happening or why), that made the difference, at least for me. I would, it turned out, undertake many flights in a wide variety of aircraft (most of them quite old) while in Viet Nam and was occasionally nervous—usually when approaching some of the small, crazy airstrips in country, but I was always reassured by the actions and demeanor of the pilots. A common theme seems to have led them to this exciting but also rather dangerous job. All else aside, each was doing this job largely because flying aircraft in the U.S. didn't offer nearly the same variety and by comparison seemed quite dull.

My trips for the WRC generally involved flying, but my ability to avoid getting into traffic accidents with the station wagon led me to occasionally run errands or deliver people from the Tin Lanh compound to some other nearby destination. I once drove a Marine chaplain, a major, onto the III MAF's extended compound. There was a well-posted speed limit, and I thought I had taken precautions by driving slowly enough. I was wrong and was signaled to pull over by an MP and did so. He came up as I rolled down the window (the station wagon was air-conditioned!), and, without so much as a word, proceeded to write me a ticket for driving 15 mph in a 10 mph zone. When he finished, the chaplain in the backseat rolled down his window and said, "Give it to me." The MP did so, and the chaplain immediately tore it into small pieces, right in front of the MP. "Let's go," he said, and off we went. I appreciated his sign of support but also spent the drive wondering just how the Marines had intended to collect the fine. If I didn't pay it, what were they going to do, send me a nasty letter through the mail? I did, however, adhere strictly to the 10 mph limit on my return trip.

My father was determined that I see as much as possible while I was there, and we took a few day trips by road. His position as the Region I education advisor meant that he visited the five provinces of the region on a regular basis. As he explained it, he spent most of his time trying to get village schools built. Education had become a U.S. priority, with funds to be allocated to build schools and then supply them with textbooks and teachers. Getting a school built was the first requirement and more difficult than it sounded, given the fact that money was not a problem, as the U.S. supplied it. That's because money actually was the problem, meaning the money that could be made from skimpy construction while selling the materials elsewhere. My father told me he had lost track of how many recently built schools he had visited only to discover that the concrete floor had been poured so thin in the middle that it cracked shortly after first being used and often disintegrated within a short time. The metal sheets used for roofing also had a substantial black market value and usually ended up arriving in fewer number than had been ordered, with still more disappearing during the construction process. Textbooks and qualified teachers were always a problem, but each needed existing schools first.

As we rode around those portions of the MRI lowlands that were "secure" during the day, we passed many typical Viet Nam scenes, among them rice paddies, pedal-driven pumps to lift water from a creek to them, and people bent over tending the rice. There were many water buffalo, and each had a young boy tending it. It was beautiful, but the reminders of war were not absent. Occasionally we passed the rusting hulks of buses or vans that had been driven over a mine and destroyed. Each had a small, makeshift memorial nearby, remembering the people who had been killed. Every time we stopped, or even slowed down around people, we were immediately confronted by boys—some quite young—running up to us, smiling and holding the first two fingers of their right hand in a V shape. This wasn't the Churchillian "victory" salute. In the Viet Nam salute the fingers were held the other way, like you hold a cigarette. Their repeated calls of "O-K, Say Lem!" made it clear what they wanted. Yet another American influence on their lives.

Refugee camps were a focus of the education effort my father was attempting to implement. The population of this northern portion of the country had, for quite some time, suffered the most frequent dislocations caused by combat. Violence had forced a substantial portion of that population to flee their homes at least once, and most were forced to resettle near the government-controlled population centers. One of the largest was in Quang Ngai Province, near the provincial capital. We toured around the site, which still housed its inhabitants in large tents. The tent sides were kept up, of course, but that lent little to what was obvious to even this first time visitor, a wretched existence for those "housed" inside.

Another, much more recent refugee camp was an objective of the one trip my father and I took together that involved both flying and driving. We flew to Quang Tri City, the capital of Quang Tri, the northernmost province in South Viet Nam. We could have taken the regional shuttle, but my father had somehow managed to get us on a C-130. That was an experience. We were allowed up front (well, almost), and the copilot gave a running commentary on what was actually a rather short flight. Just prior to arriving over Quang Tri, the pilot put us in a steep dive, in order, as he put it, to avoid the surface to air missile (SAM) sites just over the border. This was standard operating procedure, apparently. My only other time in a C-130 was a ride I hitched from Phu Bai airbase to Da Nang.

These were only two short flights, but I can say that the C-130 was the most uncomfortably noisy airplane I have ever flown in. It wasn't about the amount of the noise; I have flown in noisier. It was the nature of the noise itself, the high-pitched scream produced by the four turboprop engines. It quickly became almost aurally painful. The C-130 was designed and built to utilize short, unimproved airstrips, but it can also fly a significant distance. I could only imagine the effect of anything more than a short flight on the ears of its crew. But they wore earphones, of course.

Quang Tri City itself was located along a river (as were virtually all South Viet Nam's coastal cities). Many tragic scenes of conflict had played

Me at the intersection of Routes 1 and 9, in Quang Tri Province, just south of the DMZ, summer 1967.

out there already, and more would be in the future, up to the final collapse in 1975. Things were quiet at that moment, however. We stayed at the CORDS compound in town, as my father was a frequent visitor and well known to the advisory team. They loaned him a vehicle, and we spent two days touring this strife-torn area. Dad particularly wanted to show me the refugee camp at Cam Lo. This required us to at first drive north along Rt. 1, until we were just south of the Cam Lo River, and then turn west onto Rt. 9, which ran up into the highlands. My father stopped at the intersection and had me pose next to the signpost that showed the way to points north, including Hanoi. We were about four or five miles south of the DMZ, just below what became known as "Leatherneck Square" during years of hard fighting. I was about as far north as an American civilian could go without attracting unfavorable scrutiny, at the very least, so we went no further on Rt. 1. Rt. 9 was remarkably busy, and a substantial amount of the traffic was U.S. Army vehicles, including tanks. Following behind a tank down a dirt road in the dry season is not a pleasant experience, particularly in a vehicle that is considerably less than airtight even with the windows rolled up. I wasn't sure whether I felt safe because the tank was so near, or exposed because I was near a choice target.

Acres of agony: the Cam Lo Refugee Camp, Quang Tri Province, summer 1967.

Cam Lo was the largest refugee camp I visited during this visit, although I never got any estimate of its population. A rigid rectangle of streets and lots (the site had been prepared by U.S. engineers) was beginning to sprout simple bamboo pole frames and what I had realized by that point was the ubiquitous sign of a U.S.–inspired settlement: corrugated steel roofing sheets, used for both roofs and walls.

As we drove around this quite large project, I had the first inkling of a question that would rise to one of high importance during my second time in-country. Cam Lo gave the appearance (to a one-time, quick visitor) of a well-organized, developing community. Its residents had been driven from their homes at least once, and the chance to return to a stable farming existence was clearly to the good (assuming there was arable land nearby, which was unclear). Yet I remembered our trip there as one along a road dominated by military vehicles. This camp was just south of the DMZ. The land for miles around was spotted with Fire Support Bases (FSBs), and Camp Carroll—a Marine base—was just down a side road. If the NVA were to attack across the DMZ, this camp would be quickly untenable, regardless of the outcome of the attack itself. The camp was also directly on the path an NVA unit attacking out of Laos, off the Ho Chi Minh Trail, would follow toward Quang Tri City. Why in God's name had this site, so incredibly exposed, been selected to house people who had already suffered directly from the war? My father had no answer, of course, and I didn't ask anyone else, although I should have. I believe that this was my introduction to the central issue in the U.S./GVN attempt to "pacify" the countryside: the relationship between people and security. I would learn a great deal more about this later.

Our longest day trip during this visit was a drive down to the ancient imperial capital of Hue, in Thua Thien Province, south of Quang Tri Province. It was a day trip, of course, with more road travel than was usual, so we started somewhat earlier. I say somewhat, because part of the gallows humor in Viet Nam was remarks like "Let's wait a little before we leave, and let the locals discover where the mines were laid last night." The trip was uneventful but scenic in a manner much different from DaLat. Green was everywhere (except on the roads), but in a flat landscape in a grid of rice paddies. We had no time to drive around the city of Hue itself but went directly to the CORDS compound, located near the Perfume River, opposite the Citadel. This was a remarkable site; the Citadel itself was quite large (several square miles), and enclosed other operations, including

My father and I about to depart for Cam Lo, summer 1967. The guns were a stunt; we didn't take them.

an ARVN military headquarters and even private residences. The Citadel was surrounded by a massive masonry wall and moat, built in what looked remarkably like Classic European, Vauban style. In fact it was, and dated back only to the 19th century. Our goal was within the Citadel and close to the river, the "Forbidden City." This city-within-a-city was much older, and had had been the home of the Nguyen Dynasty emperors, where they lived cut off completely from outsiders. Access to their quarters by commoners had been forbidden. But the Nguyen emperors were long gone by then.

We parked our vehicle at the CORDS compound and walked across the river on the nearby bridge. When we reached the grounds of the inner Palace, an elderly couple let us in through a rusted gate. We were free to wander around and in fact had no other choice, as the grounds were not open to the general public. We saw no one else while we were there. It was all quite eerie. The buildings, gardens, and ponds were all laid out gracefully and appeared to be in remarkably good shape, at least from their exteriors. We could not enter any of the buildings, as all were locked. There were no signs whatsoever and no explanatory materials anywhere. We had no idea what we were looking at, but each building was beautiful, built in the slanted-roof-with-upturned-corners East Asian style. The carefully laid ponds were dry and brush-choked. Weeds poked up through gaps in the tiles that covered the grounds, but they were fewer in number and shorter than would have been the case in a totally neglected site. Maintenance was clearly not a priority, but efforts were being made. In a different world, with funding and historical research (and no war), the imperial city at Hue could have been a major tourist attraction. I left with the hope that this might be possible some day in the future, and never saw it again.[2]

Khe Sanh

In early August, Mr. Warren told me that for my next trip I would be escorting some twenty bags of cement bound for a missionary couple working in western Quang Tri Province, a few miles from the Laotian border. They were part of Wycliffe Bible Translators and were living among the Bru tribal people in the area. Their organization's purpose was to translate the Bible, and for the Bru Montagnard people this essentially meant creating a written language. The cement I would deliver was to be used for a school they would help the local people build. This was not part of any government program, but strictly a Tin Lanh one. I would accompany the cement to the airstrip nearest their home, located, luckily, only a short distance away. Once there, I was to ask for transportation to their home site. That airstrip was at a Marine base known as Khe Sanh.

Mentioning the name "Khe Sanh" got my attention. The Battle of Khe Sanh as history knows it had not yet taken place, but "the Battle of the Hills," a struggle to secure the high ground around the base in April and

May, had been well reported in American newspapers. Marine casualties had been about 150 already and were continuing. Hill 881 (actually two peaks, 881N and 881S) was already a synonym for American valor. Many brave men—on both sides—had died up there. We had, of course, abandoned the peaks as soon as they had been so dearly won but later had to send detachments back to them to keep them from being reoccupied and used against the garrison. This was risky business, as the NVA remained in the area, if not yet in the numbers they would send later. I had a little trouble wrapping my mind around the idea of a Western couple living alone in one of the most unfriendly places on earth at that time, seemingly oblivious to the fact that a real war was going on all around them. This was going to be a very interesting trip.

On the allotted day, I drove the station wagon out to the Air America terminal and parked in the lot nearby. I didn't take anything with me, because I never did unless I knew for sure the trip would be overnight, so I simply walked to the plane, a C-47, and loaded the cement bags—with help, fortunately. I gave this trip more thought than I had previous ones. My trips were always catch-as-catch-can affairs, without transportation back, but this was pushing things a bit. My arrival was supposed to have

Two of the deadly hills around the Marine base at Khe Sanh, summer 1967.

been announced to the Marines at Khe Sanh, but I had little confidence about this. As it turned out, I was right.

The flight itself was short, over rugged, verdant hillsides even more scarred by the frequency of bomb craters than had been the case in II Corps. Again there were no seats, so I half sat, half lay on the bags of cement. The Khe Sanh base itself was located in a valley, surrounded by high ground. As we made our approach down toward the airstrip, my mind flashed back to what I had read about the battle of Dien Bien Phu, and I began to see the similarities. The French had deliberately provoked a major confrontation of forces in an obscure, largely unpopulated area, believing their superior technology would defeat the massed forces of the Viet Minh. They were wrong, dead wrong. Westmoreland had done virtually the same thing (though less far away) by establishing Khe Sanh, also hoping to initiate a set-piece battle where American technology would triumph. That's where things stood at that moment. He put his faith in U.S. airpower, but, unlike the French, we were at least trying to hold the surrounding high ground.

I reported in to the airstrip HQ as the plane was unloaded. Things were quiet, but no Air America plane ever stayed any longer than it had to, so mine took off immediately. Of course no one had been informed of my arrival, so I had to explain why I was there. The Marine major at the air traffic control center (a building—actually a bunker—that did not justify its title) was not at all pleased to see me and incredulous at what I was asking him to do. "I'm gonna need two trucks and a full squad of Marines to take care of you," he growled. After some further fussing, he said, "Just sit tight. I'll see what I can do." At least he knew where the missionary couple was, it seemed. So I went back to my pile of cement bags and sat tight. For hours. I had brought my camera with me and walked around a little taking photos, but I never strayed far from my pile of cement bags. Many a Marine, either walking or driving past, had cast covetous eyes on them; it would not have been wise to leave them unobserved.

About mid-afternoon a jeep drove by, then turned around and returned to me. The driver wasn't a Marine; he was Special Forces (Green Berets) and had three Montagnard soldiers with him. He introduced himself and told me he was from the Special Forces camp at Lang Vei, not too far away. The camp had been attacked a couple of months earlier and almost overrun. They had decided to relocate it to a more defensible location, and some additional concrete would greatly help things. Things were quiet at that point, but the NVA were going to return, he was sure. He began trying to swing a deal for one or two of my bags. He opened his pitch with the holy grail of souvenir hunters, an AK-47 semiautomatic rifle "captured from the NVA." This told me how important my cement was. I was truly sorry, but I wasn't tempted. I could have had my own souvenir AK-47, plus who knows how much more if I had been cooperative, but I wasn't. The cement had been entrusted to me and I was going to see that it was delivered. He finally gave up and drove off. As he departed, I remember thinking that if the NVA were building up in this area, how long would the Wycliffe Bible couple be able to remain? Would the cement actually be used? And if so, by whom? I tried my best to shut out such thoughts.

It wasn't long afterward that two deuce-and-a-half trucks pulled up, a squad of Marines got off, and we loaded the bags of cement. Then off we went into the jungle along a small, twisty, rutted road. It wasn't a long journey, but the Marines kept a close watch, with their M-16s at the ready. I just tried to look inconspicuous, although in my civilian clothes I was the one that stuck out. We pulled into a small cleared field that had a thatch-roof bungalow at one edge. It had the floor raised as a platform and thin wood walls and was clearly built on Montagnard lines. It had neither electricity nor running water, of course. The couple who greeted us were young Americans and the wife was very pregnant. They introduced themselves as John and Carolyn Miller and made us feel welcome.[3] They thanked us for the cement and insisted we stay for something to eat. The Marines didn't want to stay long, but she quickly whipped up some tasty deep-fried dough balls, which we handed around and enjoyed. While we were there, one Marine asked about the holes in two of the walls opposite each other, and she replied lightly that yes, they had had to hit the floor that particular night as the bullets passed through.

This was all very surreal. We had to take two trucks and a squad of Marines to visit a Western couple living a marginal existence alone but for the people they were working with, serving the Lord amidst constant warfare. News from Viet Nam dominated the airwaves back home but I had never heard of these people, and I suspected very few others had either. I wanted to talk to them and learn more, but in truth I wanted to get out of the area before dark rather more. I made no objection when the sergeant in charge said we had to get going. We said our goodbyes and departed. The return journey was uneventful, and I was deposited back at the airstrip and told "good luck!" as the trucks and the Marines departed.

It was now late afternoon, and as I sat around at the airstrip that question returned: *What am I doing here*? The emphasis was on the "here" this time. I began to wonder just where I might be spending the night. This was more than an academic question. All of my previous waits had been at either province level airstrips or military bases. This was one of the latter, but the others had been headquarters and support centers, with frequent flights in and out. Time spent waiting was usually in some sort of structure, with a roof at least. This was an isolated base deep in the jungle, with no accommodations for visitors. One of the Marines who walked by stopped to talk to me and told me that his bunkmate was on leave, so there was a bunk, a flak jacket, and a helmet for me if I needed it and he told me how to find him. I thanked him, and had every intention of taking him up on his offer if it became necessary. Then, as the sun was setting behind the mountains in Laos, a Marine helicopter flew in and dropped off several passengers. It was one of the big single-rotor ones, a CH-53. I spoke to the loadmaster and he was able to fit me in, if only just. I saw no empty seats along either side as the helicopter began its ascent. Shortly after clearing the area of the camp, one of the Marines seated along my side, about six people away from me, cried out in pain. He had been hit in the leg by a bullet, which fortunately had done no further damage. It seemed to be the only bullet that struck the helicopter, at least that any of us could tell. He wasn't badly hurt, and medical supplies onboard took care of things until we were to land. That was at the Marine base at Dong Ha, as it turned out (I hadn't asked where we were going). This was better than out in the jungle, but I was really no closer to Da Nang. I was out of the danger zone, but not where I wanted to be. Fortunately, air traffic in and out of Dong Ha was extensive. I did manage to catch a ride on a C-130 back to Da Nang a short time later. After arrival, late at night, I walked to my Frontenac and drove home. It was an almost conventional end to a very long and strange day.

The Khe Sanh trip was not my last delivery by airplane, but by then I had begun to notice a problem. Bouncing around in these and several trucks had produced a literal pain in my butt. When it started to bleed, I needed to seek help, so my planned stay in Viet Nam was cut short by about ten days. Just before I left, Mr. and Mrs. Warren presented me with $100 cash as a "thank you" for my work with them. I tried mightily to demur, but they were insistent. My volunteer status thus compromised, my father scheduled my Air America flight back to Saigon.

I flew back to Saigon on a C-47 through stormy weather. In fact, it would be the roughest flight I ever took. This was the regular shuttle flight, whose sling seats along each side had no seat belts, so I had to hold on tight. Most of the others occupying the seats along each side were Vietnamese women (they had to be booked by an American man, of course) and a few children. The plane began to really bounce in all directions, as we were flying in the storm, not above it, all the way to Saigon. In the seats around me, the Vietnamese women were getting sick and vomiting onto the floor. As the plane lurched, twisted, and turned the collective vomit rolled back and forth about the floor. It was distinctly unpleasant, particularly the odor, but I survived without contributing to the mess. By that time, I was comfortable in an Air America plane, even in such weather, although I may have been the only person feeling that way on this particular flight. We arrived in Saigon eventually, and I couldn't wait to deplane.

I returned to Manila, where the embassy doctor there identified my problem as a pilonidal cyst at the base of my spine. I flew up to Clark Air

From World War II to Viet Nam. Vietnamese sheltering under the wing of the ubiquitous C-47, 1970.

Base in the Luzon highlands and had it cut out at the Air Force hospital there. The doctor employed the "leave it open and let it heal slowly while using Tucks pads to clean away the accumulated pus on a frequent basis" technique. After a few days, I was allowed to depart, although the cut had barely begun to heal. I was fortunate in that the Pan Am stewardesses were very understanding about my need to stand up for most of the flight to the States. It was back-to-school time.

Two

Back in Class Again
September 1967–June 1970

When I left Viet Nam in August of 1967 I had no plans to return. I had been given a unique opportunity to visit—in relative safety—the country that was the number one issue of the day, the focus of so much discussion and disagreement in our society. I had seized that opportunity, and its aftermath would bring about in me a fundamental reexamination of my opinions about Viet Nam and the U.S. presence there. Over the next two years, these renegade thoughts would combine with others generated by the events of those years to alter in virtually all respects my previous embrace of libertarian conservatism. They would not, however, alter my embrace, only my understanding of what it should champion.

In one very important respect, I definitely did not want to return to Viet Nam. I did not want to return there in a uniform. I had been since 1965 enjoying the middle class white guy's exemption from the draft, a college student deferment. I would graduate in June of 1969, and my fate after that date was not just uncertain, it was unknown. The draft selected and inducted men into military service through a large number of "local boards," each board proceeding on a solely local—and often distinct— manner as to selecting how many and who. The local board system had strong roots in an America that had traditionally sent its men to war via state, not federal, agency. Unfortunately, the result of each local board's acting largely on its own was a growing sea of inequities, particularly along racial lines. Calls for a solution were circulating, and one way or another I figured the issue would be decided for me. And it was.

Stuck in the Middle with...?

I was now a junior at the Georgetown University School of Foreign Service. I settled into an apartment with three other students, #1681 35th Street NW, Washington, D.C., and began a new routine of classes. It was immediately obvious that the issue of our involvement in Viet Nam had only grown while I had been away. Viet Nam was the dominant topic in both the news and among late-night campus bull sessions, although civil rights did occasionally muscle its way in. But when the subject was Viet Nam, I found myself curiously isolated. If there were any veterans among the student population of Georgetown at that time, they were keeping a low profile. Barring the theoretical existence of a veteran, I was likely the only student on campus who had actually been to Viet Nam. I had had only a taste, but it put quite a different slant on things than what I had been absorbing from the news and conversations. As I listened to the increasingly shrill rhetoric, I began to silently ask myself, "Are we talking about the same place?" On campus, Viet Nam existed only as a concept with quite different definitions, according to whatever ideological view-point the particular individual held. Ironically, these attitudes mirrored the Vietnamese/American penchant for classifying absolutely everything as either "number one!" or "number ten!" When it came to opinions about Viet Nam, there was no middle ground. But in the middle was where I found myself.

I wasn't sure at that point whether there was a "right" side to the issue, but I now believed that we were definitely on the wrong side. My reasons for that assessment were—at that point—entirely practical. My brief exposure to the country—some of it visual, but mostly from hearing stories—had suggested to me that "our Vietnamese," the GVN/ARVN, were not really interested in either good government or good warfare. Avarice was the goal of the former and incompetence the method in the latter. "Our side" was fighting a 9–5 war and buttoned themselves up every night and ignored what was happening in the areas they were supposed to secure. In considerable contrast, the other side went through hell on a regular basis just getting somewhere, then went into combat with a feroc-ity that was simply unmatched by anything on "our" side. We were expend-ing an almighty lot of dollars—and a great many lives—to sustain, in the name of anti-communism, an ineffectiveness that was so visible even I, still somewhat sympathetic, had no trouble seeing.

A Spear-Carrier in Viet Nam

My exposure to refugees and the Montagnards had also made it clear that we were causing a huge amount of damage to the people of Viet Nam in ways that extended far beyond just destruction, as excessive as that itself was. Our presence was having a massive effect on the people and culture of Viet Nam quite outside the havoc our bombs and guns were wreaking, and none of the visible signs of that presence were good. Its effect on the Vietnamese themselves was not only catastrophic but also far-reaching. Their cultural and moral values were under attack from that most hardened of foes, the almighty dollar, and they were losing that battle. As I began to examine these real issues, more and more I began to ask myself, *Why should this be?* Of course, no one was interested in what I had to say because I didn't have an emphatic, all-or-nothing opinion when this was a time for taking sides emphatically. At that point, my life goal was still what it had been before I went to Viet Nam, to take and pass the Foreign Service Exam after graduating from Georgetown and then serve— overseas, as much as possible—in the U.S. State Department. The next three years would see a fundamental change in that as well, although an entirely unwelcome one.

To a substantial degree, however, the changes in my viewpoints stemmed from the simple fact that I resided in Washington, D.C., from the fall of 1965 to June of 1970. Those were tumultuous years across the entire nation, but it certainly seemed like the focus was on the nation's capital, at least to those of use who lived there. My Ayn Rand-infused attitude toward the worth of the individual came with no qualifications, despite my upbringing in less than diverse surroundings. That is why I, not long after beginning residence in Washington, D.C., began to see the true condition of most of the people who lived there. Our nation's capital largely deserved the derisive title Georgetown students had given it: "the last plantation." Those more focused called it "the Broyhill plantation," recognizing the role of Virginia congressman Joel Broyhill in the House committee that oversaw District affairs. He had opposed just about everything proposed for the District, from school integration to home rule, for quite some time, and was still in office.

Washington, D.C.'s, African American population was in a solid majority, while its minority Caucasian population was overwhelmingly concentrated in the city's northwest quadrant. Georgetown University was comfortably ensconced within the white zone. I spent the most part of five years living there, but could count my trips into the deeply black areas of the city on the fingers of both hands, except for a brief period of employment (more about that below) deep in the northeast.

The changing conditions at Georgetown University reflected those times, although they always seemed to be more than a little bit behind. GU was—and still is, of course—a Jesuit university, and back in the 1960s those in charge of Georgetown took the phrase "in loco parentis" quite seriously. We were always addressed as the "Ladies and Gentlemen of Georgetown" (the "Ladies" part was rather recent), and respectable behavior on our part was assumed, despite steadily increasing evidence to the contrary. All Catholics had to attend religion classes, and we lesser breeds without the law had to take a required course for each of the first two years that met in the late afternoon, when all the sports teams were practicing. I always wondered about that. During my freshman year men were required to wear a coat and tie to all classes, the library, and the cafeteria. That had been the custom for some time at Georgetown, but my freshman year was the last, thank God. GU was a conservative university but found during the 1960s that its students were steadily less so. It was never Cal Berkeley, but by the time of my graduation in 1969 the school actually had a Students for a Democratic Society (SDS) chapter—not recognized by the university, of course. Most of this shift in viewpoint seemed to arrive during the last two years of my attendance there.

Georgetown University did not enjoy athletic excellence during the latter 1960s. It had cancelled its football program decades earlier, and the basketball team recruited only short, slow white guys (the team had exactly one African American player during my four years there, and he rode the bench). When I arrived, the best-attended sport was polo. At least one student (always in the School of Business Administration) had brought his string of polo ponies with him from South America and he and his compatriots played a good game. It was basically an opportunity to party in *faux* posh surroundings, and those conservative Georgetown students always found time to party.

Georgetown's varsity sport during this period, and one in which it excelled, was campus politics. This was particularly true on the East Campus. I was drawn to this immediately and enjoyed it immensely. The campus politics at Georgetown were remarkably sophisticated. This seemed to compensate for the fact that those elected had virtually no influence on the school's direction. There were two student councils, one for the college and one for the East Campus, along the time-honored principle of divide and rule. Thus more than the usual number of budding politicians could contend on a minor—but important—stage as long as they played with a skill and effort hugely disproportionate to the result. The result was a quite sophisticated political process, at least for a college campus at that time. Georgetown students were not street demonstrators (at least not initially), but were those who worked to bring about change within the system, or so we claimed.

In the spring of my sophomore year, I played a not-insignificant role in defeating one such campus politician in the SFS class ahead of me everyone had assumed was going to be elected president of the East Campus for the coming academic year. A group of us decided that this guy was way too much "Joe Hoya," always properly dressed and, at least we believed, much too subservient to "the Jebbies." He just needed to be taken down and his path to glory at least obstructed. He was clearly a natural politician, known to everyone on campus, or so it seemed. This was going to be a tough one, but that was the challenge. We couldn't out-charisma him, but we thought we could out-organize and outwork him. We found a political nobody, got him to run, and actually defeated The Anointed One, all due to the Georgetown specialty: political organization. The Anointed One's name was Bill Clinton.

The fall semester of 1967 quickly demonstrated how central Viet Nam had become to campus discourse. We learned of the "March on the Pentagon" planned for the next month, October. This presented me and my roommates (they, although more liberal than I, shared my focus on working "within the system") with a problem. Several of our friends declared their intention to join and did so. We, however, saw little point in "confronting" any opposition *on their grounds*, i.e., in the streets or at the Pentagon, seeing it as pointless, good only for salving one's soul, and not leading to any real progress. Then came the evening of the march itself. We sat in our apartment, and only one thing was discussed. It was cold and it was damp, and we knew some of the people huddled outside the Pentagon. We didn't agree with their tactics, but they were our friends, so we eventually decided we needed to help. We scrounged around and found the only food item always in stock in our larder, potatoes (home fries were a group fave). We baked all we could find, then double-wrapped them in tin foil. We put them in a car (I don't remember whose, as none of my roommates had one), and drove out to the Pentagon. We walked up closely to the ring of soldiers who had surrounded the protestors, blocking any physical contact. The protestors were huddled only a few feet away, but we couldn't get to them. So we took out the potatoes and heaved them, one by one, over the heads of the soldiers and into the crowd inside, calling them "peace grenades." Then, our consciences somewhat salved, we drove home. The fall of 1967 also quickly delivered what would turn out to be the most significant event of my life, although I did not realize it then. I had joined one of the Foreign Service School's student-run events, the Conference on the Atlantic Community, or CONTAC, during my sophomore year, and was deeply involved in planning the next conference. CONTAC had an office in the basement of an East Campus building, and it was there that I first laid eyes on a new recruit, Barbara H., a freshman in the School of Languages and Linguistics. I can still see her in my mind's eye as she looked that day.

A very young 1968 brought "the Tet Offensive," or just "Tet of 68," the massive, coordinated attack by the VC, aided by the NVA, on almost every population center in South Viet Nam. Everyone, it seems, had been caught off guard (that wasn't quite true, but almost). Cadres attacked MACV headquarters across the grounds of the Saigon Golf Club, and a few managed to fight their way into the U.S. embassy itself. Things seemed to hang in the balance for a few days, and for me no news was good news. My father was living in Da Nang during the attack, and I had heard nothing. This was good because my mother—and in turn I—would have been contacted had my father been hurt or killed, and neither of us were. I later asked him how close the attackers in Da Nang came to his building and was told "a few blocks." He was very nonchalant about it. The chaos of the Tet Offensive was the principal news subject during the first week of February for most people at least, but my attention was distracted when the newspapers reported that the Special Forces base at Lang Vei, near Khe Sanh, had been attacked and overrun. The NVA assault on Lang Vei began a week after the opening of the Tet Offensive and during the ongoing struggle for Khe Sanh itself. This latter factor led the Marines to decline a Special Forces request for troop support against the NVA attack. For fear of ambush, they declined to make a short road trip comparable to the one I had made some seven months earlier. From my memory of that trip, they had cause to be concerned. The distance was short, but the route was a narrow dirt road, hardly more than a track, with the vegetation closing in all around, more or less textbook conditions for an ambush.

This attack was quickly reported to be the first use by the NVA of tanks, and my mind drifted back to those bags of cement I had so zealously shepherded to their destination. I thought back more than once to the Green Beret who had tried to trade for a bag or two, citing the inevitable attack that was coming. He had only briefly mentioned his name in the beginning, and I didn't note it. Was he among those killed? I began to wonder whether I should have given him one or more of the bags. With Khe Sanh not only under regular artillery attack but also surrounded by NVA regulars, I was pretty sure that the missionary couple to whom I had delivered the full load of cement bags were no longer there. Had they even been able to use the cement? A bag or two more wouldn't have made much of a difference for the garrison at Lang Vei. Still...

I had arrived for my junior year at Georgetown knowing that I would need to obtain a part-time job rather quickly, and one that paid better than those I had done so far. I concentrated on my studies during my freshman year but had discovered, to my surprise, that I had arrived on campus with a marketable skill. I could make some money from the simple fact that I could type. This was the entirely unexpected result of my not wanting to work very hard during the second semester of my senior year in high school. I had to take something, so I took a typing class. In truth, I needed to, as my cursive handwriting was pretty much illegible, and I had been informed by one of my teachers—himself a SFS graduate—of the amount of writing I would have to do. My exams would be exclusively essays, written in the infamous "blue books," and I would be writing a number of papers (and so it turned out to be). So I took the class along with one other guy and twenty-some girls. My sole male classmate was a junior who was as determined as I not to do much work and was beginning a year earlier. Sensing a common connection, we became good friends. We all sat at Olympia manual typewriters, each bolted to long benches, held our hands in the proper position just above the keyboard, and learned to "touch type." I got razzed by the guys for taking this class and was asked if I was planning to join "the steno pool," as the inevitable future of women who could type was known then, and so on.

Freshman year at Georgetown was my revenge. Many other students who either possessed handwriting as bad as mine or simply sought the boost a clean, typed paper might give would pay someone to type it for them. I earned 25 cents a page and was allowed to make two typos per page. It wasn't the kind of job I wanted to do more than occasionally, however, so I did not market myself much beyond my dorm. But it helped. I did manage to obtain a part-time job in the library by the beginning of my sophomore year. The job helped, but the fact that it was in the gorgeous old library in the Healy Building is what I remember. Once you entered, it was an awesome sight, stretching up three very tall stories. The books were stored in the walls of towering shelves, accessed by narrow walkways with only brass railings to keep books (or worse) from crashing down several levels to the floor. We who worked the shelves received our books from the returns shelf via dumbwaiters and then threaded our way down the walkway to properly place them. It was magnificent, and by that time utterly inadequate for the student body. A new, purpose-designed, soulless modernistic building, with far greater capacity and accommodations for the electronic machines just then beginning to access libraries, was under construction not far away from the Healy Building during my last year there, but I never had to use it. I consider myself fortunate.

Typing and work in the library were all well and good, but by this time my social life required that I make more money, so I began to look around. In early 1968 I ran across an ad in the *Washington Post* for young men to work at a clothing store. I had no experience in this at all and certainly no taste for clothes or fashion, but the pickings were slim, so I applied. Rather to my surprise, the store manager hired me. Part of the surprise was the store's location, deep in Northeast Washington, in a virtually all-black neighborhood. It was a bit of a trip but could be made by bus, so I accepted. The store was small and catered to young black men. The manager—who was black—got right to the point when he began training me and the other young white guy he had hired. He had hired us, he said, because his customers liked to have a white guy serving them. That made them vulnerable. They would come into the store with a few bucks for a shirt or maybe just a tie or socks. Our job was to play on their vanity and tell them how good they would look in that, but they would be so much sharper if they added a pair of pants, a belt, or whatever. We were to keep going until we had them committed to an entire outfit except for shoes (which the store didn't sell). Then we got them to give up their cash on layaway and leave with neither their money nor the item they had come in for but dreaming of that cool outfit the white guy had helped them pick out. I soon discovered that I was disturbingly good at the job. I made a silent vow to leave the moment something better came along. As things turned out, I found another reason to leave.

On the evening of April 4, 1968, both of us white guys were working the store and were scheduled to be there until closing time. Then the manager came in and called us together. If it is possible for a black man to be "ashen-faced," he was. He got right to the point. "Guys," he said, "Martin Luther King has just been shot. You two need to get out of here right now. I called a cab for each of you." We both laid low until the cabs came and then tried to enter them inconspicuously when the manager signaled us to go. When the driver of my cab saw me get in the backseat, he said, "Son, you lie down on the floor and don't you get up for any reason until I say so." I did as he said. Our trip was uneventful if not comfortable. My view was pretty much limited to the not-too-clean floor mat I lay on. After what seemed like a very long ride, my driver let me get up and not too long afterward dropped me off near Dupont Circle. I gave him everything I had in my wallet.

Rioting began that night, and by the next morning the National Guard had been called in and began to arrive. I believe that martial law was never formally declared, but that evening a curfew was, enforced by the National Guard. My roommates and I at the 1681 Club got to watch as the grounds of the private school just across the street (and just north of the GU campus) became a National Guard headquarters. Numerous army deuce-and-a-half trucks and Jeeps were parked across there, with much coming and going.

Later that evening I had what must count as one of the dumbest ideas I have ever had—and that's saying something. It may not actually have been my idea (my memory is hazy on that), but if it wasn't then I agreed much too readily. Whichever it was, the source, a friend I shall call Bob, and I decided to go out into the neighborhood and check out what was happening. Never mind the curfew. I believe alcohol was involved, but not enough, as we both were able to go. We darkened our faces with burnt cork (really!), donned dark clothing and knit caps, and set out. With the National Guard across the street it was fortunate that we had a back door. We tried to be inconspicuous, but when you are the only ones outside, it doesn't feel that way. We had only one close call, and that was when we heard a vehicle approaching from around the corner and had to dive head-first over a hedge in the hope that there was nothing very hard or sharp on the other side. There wasn't, and the jeep passed us by. We had no actual destination but worked our way southward toward the P Street bridge, the major east-west connector street in that vicinity.

Some geographic information will help here. Washington, D.C., is essentially a square set on end with its southwest quadrant almost obliterated by a curve in the Potomac River. Rock Creek is a tributary that proceeds through northwest Washington in a roughly southeasterly direction until it enters the Potomac. Although Rock Creek's valley peters out by the time it reaches the Potomac, its sides are quite steep and rugged farther up the creek and bridges to cross it fewer. The P Street bridge was one of those. When I lived in Washington, Rock Creek was the geographic boundary that separated black from white. The vast majority of the white residents lived west of Rock Creek. There was a sort of "mixed" area, with Rock Creek its definite western boundary and Dupont Circle its much less definitive eastern one. A wide variety of races and nationalities lived between those two.

Bob and I worked our way toward the bridge, until we abruptly realized we should definitely not go any farther. On the western end of the P Street Bridge sandbags had been piled into a curved tactical position, with the wings sheltering soldiers inside. Three or four soldiers were there, clustered around something that neither Bob nor I could clearly see, and looking eastward down the bridge. Was it actually a machine gun? I thought so at the time but also knew that I just wasn't sure, given the darkness and the distance, and could not swear to it in court. But that made sense, from a military point of view that was beyond obvious, even to us civilians. The national guard had deployed all over the city and was patrolling the streets after curfew, enforcing the curfew. We presumed the guard was protecting the capital buildings, which were much closer to the rioting than we were. But it was also protecting the "White Ghetto" from attack by the black masses to the east. The sandbagged position had quite obviously been placed to repel an attack across the bridge from east to west, i.e., from black to white. Rock Creek's sides along the stretch around P Street were very steep, so the only way such an attack could proceed was across a bridge. Hold at the bridge and the white people behind would be safe. Almost fifty years later this seems like a sweeping conclusion from a pretty partial viewpoint, but given the emotional climate of the time it seemed quite reasonable to think like that. I wish I had been able to see what the Pennsylvania Avenue or M Street bridges looked like.

I stopped working at the clothing store; in fact, I never went there again after that night. Just a short time later, however, I found the very best part-time job available in the District of Columbia. I began to work at the Cellar Door, a nightclub on M Street at 34th Street, quite close to the GU campus. That proximity meant that GU students had the inside track to get a job, and I heard of an opening early enough to get there first. Working at the Cellar Door was definitely a work-your-way-up-the-ladder type of thing. I began as a doorman, then graduated to doing the lights and sound for the acts. A week spent trying to light Anthony and the Imperials convinced me I had no business doing the lights and sound, but fortunately I was asked to become the club bartender. This was a critical job, as the club had a service bar that got obscenely busy when the house "turned over," i.e., the previous audience departed and was quickly replaced by an entirely new audience that had been waiting outside. The pay was reasonably good, as a service bar meant no tips. The work was quite stressful, however, and on a busy night I would be up to my elbows in alcohol. It also turned me against hard liquor.

But tending bar was not and never had been my goal. Like everybody else, I wanted to be a waiter. Waiters made the real money. The pay was lousy, of course, but the tips could be quite substantial, depending on the audience. The money was good, but the real point was that waiters got paid to listen to some of the country's premier musical and comedic talent, up close and personal, in a small, intimate venue. I eventually graduated to waiter and loved the job so much I remained in D.C. for the summer between my junior and senior years and kept the job for a year after being hired by USAID, while in training across the river in Roslyn, Virginia. I left only when I absolutely had to.

The acts were the real attraction, as the club featured folk, jazz, pop, and comedy. But there were side benefits also. Hearing that the club needed a location for the occasional late Saturday night party with the performer of the week, I volunteered the 1681 Club on the spot, an offer my roommates unanimously supported post facto. Thus we got to host the likes of Gordon Lightfoot, Ian and Sylvia, and, believe it or not, Rick Nelson. The latter didn't actually party with us. Our doorman had recruited two young women in the audience at the last show to join us, and the star spent the entire time in a bedroom with them. Sometimes the performers were friendly, and liked to hang around with the staff. I got to drink beer with Tom Rush, take Red Shea (Gordon Lightfoot's guitarist) around northern Virginia on the back of my motorcycle in search of a particular guitar string, and play softball with Richard Pryor. The memories will live with me forever.

The trigger for all that would follow my graduation was the announcement that there would be no Foreign Service Officer (FSO) exam that year, and there might not be one for the foreseeable future. The FSO exam is a complex, difficult one, with both a written and a verbal component. I had wanted to be an FSO before getting drafted became an issue, but becoming an FSO meant an exemption from the draft, at least for a very few. Those aspiring to it were probably also a small number, but that number had grown quite a bit and the backlog of those who had passed the test but still awaited appointments had grown to the point that no new exams were going to be scheduled. I had to find another plan, and at that point graduate school held no appeal for me. I was in love and planning to get married, so I looked around at other possibilities in government service, even the CIA. I do not recall the specifics of how I applied to USAID to serve in Viet Nam. With the State Department temporarily out of reach, by joining USAID I could stay in the loop and accumulate some experience for another try later. So I applied. I stressed my Viet Nam summer in my application, of course, in particular the trips to various places delivering relief supplies. My experience was, as I phrased it, "limited but relevant," and USAID agreed, more than I appreciated at first.

My immediate future became clearer when I received a letter officially appointing me to a USAID post as an "Assistant Relief/Rehabilitation Officer," to serve in Viet Nam. This testified to the relevancy of my experience, but my formal designation as an FSR/L-8 testified to its limited nature. The FSR rank chain was identical to the FSO in numbers, status, and pay, although it did not carry the career guarantee. An eight was the lowest possible rank of an AID officer. My starting salary, if memory serves, was about $6,800 per year.

The "/L" was the really significant part of the job title. It meant "limited." The /Ls had been hired specifically for service in Viet Nam, with no expectation of service elsewhere, and could be terminated at any point. That was made clear to us, and I accepted the job with that knowledge. I had thus been handed my own personal method of taking a middle path down the Viet Nam highway. I had no desire to go and contribute to the massive—and massively ineffective—destruction being wreaked on that poor land, but I realized that as an "Assistant Relief/Rehabilitation Officer" I would be working to aid the most unfortunate of all the unfortunate people of Viet Nam, those who had been forced to flee their homes and consigned to huddle in makeshift refugee camps. I did not wish to "serve" in Viet Nam, but neither was I going to hide from the unpleasant reality to which I had been introduced. This was an opportunity to do something positive, I thought. I was not just willing but actually enthusiastic about going there to help those uprooted by the conflict. There was one major downside to all that idealism, and I was already aware of it, or at least I thought I was. My work helping suffering people would have to be conducted indirectly. I would be an "advisor," working to make sure that my counterpart in the GVN—whomever that might be—did the job he was supposed to do. I was already aware that exerting our supposed authority among the government we were "helping" was difficult. Anyone who read the newspapers or watched the evening news knew that by now. But I had much more to learn, and that learning began a couple of weeks after my graduation when I began the training my job appointment required.

Once I knew my immediate future, Barbara and I planned to spend it together, regardless of the obstacles that stood in our way. We were planning to get married at the end of August, and thus I had to confront the choice that every married CORDS employee—including my father—was required to make: take an 18-month appointment and be alone, during which I could fly home every six months, or take my wife to one of the designated "safe haven" locations for dependents and have my tour extended to two years.[1] The idea of our seeing each other only every six months was out of the question, so Barbara resolved to travel with me. But she was not going to remain in some safe haven. She had decided on the Georgetown School of Languages and Linguistics because she wanted to travel and live overseas—and not just in safety. We decided on a two-step plan: first, to formally take her to safe haven in Manila, to stay with my mother. She would then obtain a job with a private contractor in Saigon. We wouldn't be together (I had absolutely no idea where I would be), but we wouldn't be half a globe apart, either.

I had no way of knowing it at the time, but I had signed on with CORDS just as things were beginning to wind down in Viet Nam. We had already decided we had won and were preparing to withdraw and leave the GVN and ARVN to take over and carry on. The necessary contraction had already begun, although it could be seen only in a few locations at that point. Within two years, that contraction would be in full swing, in the era of "Vietnamization"; but in the meantime Barbara and I would encounter clues that what we had inadvertently resolved to do was to swim upstream, against the bureaucracy. The first hint came when I applied to have my "dependent" safe-havened in Manila, Philippines. The reply came back "No," with the explanation that a freeze had been placed on new home rentals for Viet Nam dependents. In other words, there was no place for her to live, at least in the Philippines. This little wrinkle in the 18/24 decision I was required to make had not been explained to me.

We had the answer well in hand, however, as it had been part of our original plans. Barbara would not need her own residence, as she would live with my mother, who by then was residing alone in our large house in Makati, Rizal, as both my brothers had graduated from the International School and gone to college. The AID personnel department passed this on to AID Manila, and some back and forth argument ensued. I was able to read some of it (the correspondence was terse, as it travelled by cable) and saw that AID Manila was actually arguing that our idea violated the spirit of the directive, which was to reduce U.S. dependents in the Philippines. I viewed this as a narrowly bureaucratic point of view, a decision made on paper and without reference to the specific circumstances. This would not be my last encounter with such an attitude. We actually won that first battle. Permission was granted—reluctantly, to be sure—for Barbara to live in Manila with my mother. But Manila was not our goal. Saigon was.

The 18/24-month alternative also did not include the period of our Washington-based training. This program varied in length for its different participants, but as I was hired as a "language officer," I would spend a full year attending the general portions of the program followed by language training. I began in June 1969, just after graduation from the SFS. Neither of us could miss our respective classes, so Barbara and I used the Labor Day weekend that year to get married. We had a very traditional ceremony in Newtown Square, her family's hometown. Due to our far-flung status, no member of my family was able to attend my wedding, and we simply drove back to the apartment we had rented, near Dupont Circle, and got on with our lives.

VTC

The Vietnam Training Center (VTC) was a temporary operation run by the Foreign Service Institute. Traditionally, military and civilian personnel going to Viet Nam were given separate training courses, in separate locations. By the time I joined, a combined school for both civilians and military personnel had been established in Roslyn, Virginia, just across the Key Bridge from Georgetown. The VTC occupied an oddly shaped building adjoining another one. I learned later that it had been a parking garage, which explained why we went between floors on large ramps. Everyone destined for Viet Nam advisory service, whether military or civil, attended classes at VTC. When I say "military," I refer to those military personnel slated to become either a province senior advisor or a district senior advisor. These officers—and civilians—were destined to join the combined military-civilian effort known as CORDS. The military men would advise ARVN officers who were serving in GVN administrative positions in the provinces. American military men designated to advise ARVN units were not trained at VTC. The VTC had evidently been in existence for some time, as it numbered its classes, and I became a member of CORDS 20, which was always rendered as CORDS XX. Either way, we were the 20th such class.

Military personnel were by far the largest component of CORDS XX. They all held the rank of major, save one colonel, and were slotted for district senior advisor (DSA) positions. The Colonel was to be a province senior advisor (PSA). Every one of the majors was a "tanker" from the armored branch. It took me a while to realize this, and I did not inquire further as to the reason for it. It raised questions on just how the army obtained those "volunteers" for the CORDS program. We civilians were far fewer, but we were more diverse. So diverse, in fact, that classification by source was difficult then, and impossible now. Some were ex-military, some were ex-Peace Corps, some were actually FSOs (not there entirely voluntarily), and others were hired from wherever. I was one of this last group. All of them—except me—were slotted for deputy district senior advisor positions. I was the sole refugee advisor in the class. I was also CORDS XX's youngest member. I was quite obviously younger than any of the military members, and a quick study convinced me I was the youngest civilian. Every other member of my class had "work experience" in some form or another. I was the sole individual coming directly out of an undergraduate education. The ex-Peace Corps guys made the biggest impression on me, young men going willfully from one extreme of American foreign aid to another.

The basic course—mandatory for all—was six weeks long. After that, another CORDS class entered behind us, and so on every six weeks. After the military members had departed, the very much smaller group of language officers—all young civilians—would remain to complete a year of study. Language instruction began immediately, but as the vast majority of each class was going to be there for only six weeks, the level of that instruction differed between the large majority and the language officers. Lectures, followed by question-and-answer sessions, characterized most of the class time, but there was a wide variety of input, including films. All such classes, except language, were attended by both military and civilians.

Most of the presentations during the first six weeks were about the nuts-and-bolts components of "advising" someone from a different culture, all offered by Americans who had experience doing just that. This, in turn, meant how you were to get your counterpart to actually do his job. I do not say this out of later-acquired pique; that was the open attitude of all those former advisors who spoke to us. Each of those USAID officers offering non-language classes had experience as an advisor in different parts of the country, but their message was unanimous: we weren't actually going to be "advisors." Our counterparts will know what they should do; it's our job to get him to do it. The parallel MACV structure at the province and district level could provide some leverage, but the real source of our power was the American supply system, which provided almost all of the things a counterpart would want. If your counterpart won't listen to your "advice," in the words of one such veteran, you could "cut off his water." After six weeks of such presentations, we certainly had few illusions about what we were walking into. There was no session on the history of Viet Nam during these six weeks and nothing at all on the Paris Peace Conference and subsequent U.S. actions. We had enlisted as soldiers in a type of war and were training in how to win it. No one tried to justify anything.

Sadly, in this 20th attempt to meld civilians and military personnel into one smooth-running organism, it did not take too long for differences between the military and the civilian components to manifest themselves. All the civilians, regardless of their backgrounds (including ex-military) were clearly *civilians* and shared at least a point of view in common, despite their disparities. So did the military, of course, and it was all too often an opposite and increasingly antagonistic one. Things could largely be contained while we were at VTC, but the class also attended other events at other locations. The memorable week CORDS XX spent at Fort Bragg, North Carolina, produced a blowup. It definitely marred an amazing experience.

A Spear-Carrier in Viet Nam

We all flew down to Fort Bragg, and for five days were treated to the best military briefings and show-offs money could buy, courtesy of the John F. Kennedy School for Counterinsurgency Warfare. We got to vicariously experience warfare but slept in comfortable beds at night. The experience was nothing special for our military (or ex-military) members, of course, but for us civilians it was fascinating, on several levels.

By the end of the week I decided to christen the experience "101 Ways to Kill Myself." We were briefed on, treated to demonstrations of, and sometimes given the experience of actually firing a number of weapons. I learned to field strip a 45-caliber pistol and fired an M-16 on full automatic (briefly), but my favorite weapon was the M79 grenade launcher. After a talk and a demonstration, we were each given two grenades to fire at a derelict tank out on the range. I put my second shot right on the turret's face. The instructor gave me a very quizzical look (my hair hung down almost to my shoulders by that point).

But the most memorable class was the one about a weapon we were not allowed to fire but were going to become very well acquainted with, the Claymore mine. The talk opened with a bang—a loud one—as the speaker fired one off while snapping to attention and first speaking to his assembled audience. What followed was a detailed, and ultimately hilarious, talk about this singular weapon. The Claymore (named after the ancient Scottish sword) was/is an independent, "command fired" rectangular block of plastic. Curved on its long axis, the plastic encased a number of small steel balls embedded in C-4 explosive. Fold-out legs allowed it to be stuck into the ground and angled upward. It could be fired by either command over a wire or by disturbing a trip wire. It was a one-use shotgun, with very nasty results for anyone within its fan-shaped dispersal pattern of up to about 60 yards away.

Claymores were universally used as perimeter defense at MACV and ARVN installations, our speaker explained. Once set in place and wired, they didn't have to be tended; they just did the job indiscriminately when their fuse was pulled. Our instructor went into some detail outlining how tricky this actually was because we had a tricky enemy. Each convex front had the obvious label about "this side to the enemy," so placing them around your perimeter was pretty routine, he said. The problem was keeping them that way. It seems the VC/NVA would persistently crawl—very carefully—to the mines themselves (thus avoiding the trip wires that were often also in place), and instead of removing them they would reverse them, so the damage side was pointed to your camp. This was always discovered, of course, before it could deliver its nasty surprise (at least by U.S. units; there was some talk among our group that the ARVN were often too lazy to check). The initial answer, our instructor said, was to paint white Xs on the concave side, so you could see if they had been turned around. Once you did so, he said, you soon discovered that the other side had snuck up again, turned the Claymores around and painted their own Xs. This kind of move/countermove continued, descending into some complexity, as the speaker revealed the step-by-step process of an intricate game of wits. I enjoyed every minute of the presentation while hoping to never actually see a Claymore in action.

Unfortunately, one of our civilian members decided to wear a private set of fatigues each day during this week. His most unmilitary appearance, his clothes not "properly pressed," and sans any form of identification, of course, aroused some of our military classmates to indignation. To be fair, several didn't see the reason for such a fuss, but our director called a general class meeting to discuss our internal dissension. I don't recall that it helped much. You must keep in mind that several of our civilian class members (including me) wore their hair almost to their shoulders and were other in ways the antithesis of military attitude, so the problem cannot be laid solely at the feet of our member who chose to wear fatigues. I remember reflecting during the class meeting—and afterward—that if the entire CORDS approach was to meld military personnel and civilians into a team, then CORDS XX was demonstrating some potential problems. After six weeks, the large majority of CORDS XX departed for their assignments, while we few "language officers" began the year-long process of learning the Vietnamese language. Overall, the experience was reminiscent of high school, as each day we proceeded from classroom to classroom on a fixed schedule. The major difference was that, despite our frequent change in classrooms and instructors, the subject was always the same.

The VTC had a very officious director, an American man, while the director of the language instructors was Vietnamese. Our language director would periodically gather us together and have us speak, to critique our pronunciation and grasp of the tones. All of the classroom instructors were women. They varied in age, with some of them young "Cos" and others "Bas" (*Co* designates an unmarried woman, and *Ba* a married one), including one instructor who was anxious for us to realize that despite her somewhat advanced age she was to be addressed as "Co." Every instructor always wore an *ao dai* and conducted each class solely in Vietnamese. No English was spoken in any classroom. There was a textbook of sorts, but it comprised solely "dialogues" in Vietnamese with the English translation. The dialogues began quite simply and progressed in difficulty throughout our time there. During the latter months of the course the textbook was often discarded, and we discussed specific topics with each instructor.

While we began each lesson by reciting a written dialogue, reading Vietnamese composed only a very small part of the course. It was all about speaking, rightly so, but learning more about how to actually read the language would have been helpful. I say that because the gap between the sounds of Vietnamese and how they are rendered in written form is remarkably wide. The basis for this is the fact that Vietnamese is a derivative of Chinese and was for most of its existence a pictograph language, i.e., it did not use the Western concept of letters but small drawings to convey meaning. Beginning in the 17th century, Vietnamese was rendered into Western letters by Jesuits in the service of the French colonists. This westernized "National Language" (*Quoc Ngu*) gradually replaced the old system and became a symbol of national unity in the struggle against the colonialists. Speaking strictly for myself, I believe that whoever was responsible for rendering Vietnamese into a Western alphabet could have done a better job. This sounds strange coming from a native speaker of a language with some ridiculous spelling-pronunciation dilemmas, but these English problems arose over a long period of time as the language developed. Vietnamese in the Western alphabet was, in comparison, effectively invented on the spot and delivered whole. Some of the renderings in the *Quoc Ngu* defied logical explanation to me and my classmates, although probably not to the trained linguists who developed our program of study.

The Vietnamese language has astonishingly little grammar, and it can be learned quickly. There is neither number nor tense, for example. Whether the event is in the past, present, or future is entirely dependent on its context. As far as grammar goes, once you have mastered the concept of *duoc*, which has no counterpart in English, things are easy. The vocabulary, however, is something else.

The *Quoc Ngu* employs the standard Western alphabet, but with some wrinkles. Principal among these is that the Vietnamese alphabet has twenty-nine letters. Twelve of these are vowels, and seventeen are consonants. But those are just the single consonants; there are also eleven combinations of two consonants, called "consonant clusters." One of the consonant clusters became the bane of American news anchors everywhere. That was "*ng*," because just about every other Vietnamese government official was named "Nguyen" something or other. Nguyen van Thieu, who became president, and Nguyen cao Ky, who became his vice president (and who were not related), are but two examples. Virtually everyone in America pronounced "Nguyen" as some slight variation of "New-yen," making it a two syllable word. Unfortunately, Vietnamese is a monosyllabic language. It just so happens that Ng is produced by doing the exact opposite of how we pronounce the letter *n*. Instead of putting the tip of your tongue up against the back of your upper front teeth then releasing both your tongue and some air, as you do to pronounce the letter *n*, "ng" is pronounced by placing your tongue against the back of your lower front teeth and doing the same thing. Easy to say, not so easy to do. As a default, pronounce "Nguyen" as "Win"; that's close enough.

But exhibit #1 for my point about written Vietnamese is that the word most often pronounced by those in authority, from government to the press, and thus the most often mispronounced, is *Viet* itself. The Vietnamese *t* is actually pronounced as a *k*, so the word is rendered as "Ve-eck." I never met an American who was not a graduate of the Vietnamese course who knew that then or knows it now. Once you add the problems caused by the tones (see below), "Viet" had to be, ironically, the Vietnamese word most mispronounced by Americans.

That substantial gap between spelling and pronunciation also led to what was easily the most embarrassing moment CORDS XX's language officers encountered during our time there. It was late in our training, when we were past the dialogues and simply following the instructor's lead in discussing a subject. One class, led by one of the better-looking instructors, who was both young and delicate, with her ao dai emphasizing her hourglass waist, began with her announcing that she was going to talk about Buddhism in Vietnamese life. This is a rather central topic, as Buddhism is the dominant religion among the Vietnamese (although not among the leaders of the GVN; they were usually Catholic). We all knew what was coming, but that didn't help. She began, and all was well for a few minutes. Then, as she continued to speak, the urge to giggle and then laugh welled up in me, despite my best efforts. I looked furtively around the room and realized that everyone was just like me, trying to restrain themselves and becoming steadily less effective at it. It was just too damn funny. Then the point came when the entire class broke down in laughter. She stopped, both mystified and indignant, and asked why we were behaving like that. In Vietnamese, Buddha—as well as Buddhism and Buddhist—is spelled "*Phat.*" Phat however, is pronounced exactly like "fuck." Thus it was that our class, despite knowing this fact, could resist for only so long the incongruity of a beautiful young woman speaking to us and having about every third word out of her dainty little mouth be "fuck." Needless to say, none of us volunteered to explain to her why we were laughing so hard.

The large number of vowels and consonant clusters were a problem, but, as we were speaking and not writing, the real problem came from the fact that we native English speakers were trying to learn a tonal language. Vietnamese is rightly referred to as a tonal language, but so, in a way, is English. The problem is that Vietnamese is *word tonal*, while English is *sentence tonal*. Consider, for example, how many different moods you can demonstrate in English simply by saying the words "come in." Feelings ranging from joyous welcome, through disinterest to open antagonism can be expressed simply by changing the tone of those same two words. English speakers also have natural, unconscious, tonal components to their phrases and sentences. The most important to us as aspiring Vietnamese speakers was the insidious tonal characteristic of English speakers, speaking the last syllable of each phrase or sentence in a *declining* tone. Listen to yourself carefully, and you will hear this at virtually every pause of speaking, whether comma or period. It's subtle, and happens at the very end of the last syllable we speak, but it causes a big problem because it's automatic to us; we don't recognize we are doing it. The declining tone is one of the Vietnamese language's five tones, and while some sentences thus end with a declining tone, most don't. Native English speakers tend to render their Vietnamese with this common characteristic, causing considerable problems.

Written Vietnamese actually has six tones, five of them produced by a mark over or below the word.[2] Tone One has no mark. But we were taught only five tones. We were told that even the Vietnamese did not differentiate in their speaking between two of the tones. This was small comfort, because we quickly learned that "just" five tones presented us with the same huge problem: if we don't hit the tone exactly right, we aren't just mispronouncing the word, we are saying *an entirely different word*. Tone One is called—in Vietnamese—"no tone," but it definitely has one, and it cannot be allowed to drop or waver, because that would make it another tone. Tone Two is a rising tone and easily the most difficult one to hit correctly. I discovered that if I mentally phrase the word as a question, emphasizing the "?," I could produce the rising tone. Tone Three required a waver, a drop then a rise, and it must end on the rise, despite an English speaker's tendency to let it one decline at the end. Tone Four is the declining tone, the easiest one for an English speaker to employ. Tone Five is also a declining tone but one that must be caught and restricted and not allowed to continue down, like Tone Four. I found this an unpleasant sound, quite guttural, and was always conscious of this, even as I did my best to imitate it.

Together, the new letters and the tones conspired to make the learning process a difficult one. We kept at it, all day every day, for several months after the others had left, but none of us ever felt we had mastered it. Traps lay everywhere, even in the simplest and most often used words and phrases. *Chao*, pretty much the first word everyone learned, was a deceptively easy beginning. It means "Hello" and is pronounced the same as the Italian "Ciao" or the English "chow." It's also the fourth—dropping—tone and thus the easiest for an English speaker to adopt. Chao was usually followed by perhaps the most frequently occurring word in our study, *ong*. It means man, and, despite its spelling, is rendered as "om," rather like in Transcendental Meditation. It is in the first, "no" tone, but you must hit and not drop it at the very end. One of its plural forms—that used in direct address to a group—was *Cac Ong*, which means All Men (yes, Vietnamese is as patriarchal as English). Cac had to be rendered in the rising tone, then ong in the "no" tone. The real problem was the American unfamiliarity with ending a word with a hard consonant followed by one with a soft vowel. Each of us language officers, over the entire period of our study, continued to struggle with this essential phrase. Our Vietnamese language program supervisor would periodically meet with us and have us recite those two words. Despite our best efforts, a Vietnamese was probably going to hear us say not "*Chao cac ong*," but "*Chao ca com*," which means "Hello, fish and rice."

A related, if somewhat more salacious, issue arose over the Vietnamese currency. It was the "*dong*," which was properly pronounced "dom," but of course, saying the wrong word was extremely easy. To avoid this, absolutely every American I met called the currency a "piaster," which is the French term. Or consider the title each of us was to bear: "*Co Van*

65

My." Co Van meant "advisor," and was pronounced "Caw Vyung," with both words in the second—rising—tone. *My* meant American, and thus was a word we expected to use frequently. It is pronounced me, with the down-and-up third tone. If we didn't come back up, falling victim to the universal American vice of dropping the tone at the very end of a statement, then we identified ourselves as *My,* a form of rice noodle. It appears that no one, with the very sparse exception of us language officers, whether in government or the media, paid much attention to even the basic principles of the Vietnamese language, including tones or even basic pronunciation. The above gives you a brief introduction to the pitfalls that lurk for the unprepared. What follows is an example.

From the early days of our language classes, we heard a story about how Secretary of Defense McNamara had embarrassed himself by attempting to speak Vietnamese in public. It was while he was on a visit to Saigon to consult with General Khanh, the then-current winner in the musical governments coup-and-coup-again period in the GVN government. General Khanh was short and fat and always wore a beret and sunglasses in public. McNamara was scheduled to make a short public appearance with General Khanh, and someone on his staff apparently decided that it would be great if the Secretary would say a few words in Vietnamese to the wholly Vietnamese (except for the press, of course) audience before which he was going to appear. They decided on the phrase "Vietnam Forever!" This phrase is rendered in Vietnamese as four words, *"Viet Nam Muon Nam,"* and actually means Viet Nam Ten Thousand Years. This presented several problems. The first is that Vietnamese, just like English, has some words that mean entirely different things according to the context in which they appear. *"Nam"* is one of them. Spoken in Tone One, it means "year," or "south," according to the context.[3] Spoken in Tone Four, it means "lie down." No one apparently told him this, but it would be only part of his undoing.

During the ceremony, thinking himself prepared, Secretary McNamara dutifully took General Khanh's hand at the prescribed time, held it aloft with his (which had to have been difficult, given the difference in their heights), and spoke four words. His audience, duly impressed, applauded vigorously. Unfortunately, the secretary committed four mistakes in those four words, which had him saying something entirely different from what he thought he was saying. He got things off to a bad start when he followed Lyndon Johnson's example and pronounced "Viet" as

"Vit." In Vietnamese, "*vit*" is a duck. He did get the first "Nam" right (or close enough), but because context is important that only made things worse. By getting "Nam" right, he actually said, " A southern duck." Then he made two mistakes on the third word. English speakers, particularly when orating in public, feel compelled to emphasize some words strongly. It usually involves raising the tone of one's voice, and McNamara did it here. The last three words, "*Nam muon nam*," are all Tone One and must be hit the same. But McNamara emphasized "*muon*" (rather like politicians often declare that we "MUST!" do something). That made it Tone Two, which, combined with a slight mispronunciation (an easy one to make, I admit), made him say "*Muong*," which meant "wants to." Then he capped it off by committing that most common of all errors: dropping the tone of the last syllable. "Nam" came out as a descending tone, meaning "to lie down." For a long time, I considered the tale to be questionable and quite possibly apocryphal. Then, quite late in the language course, I saw the video of his appearance with General Khanh and understood exactly what he did say. I can therefore testify that U.S. Secretary of Defense Robert McNamara once travelled halfway around the world, grasped his host country's leader by the hand, and told his assembled audience, "A southern duck wants to lie down."

My by-now monotonous daily routine suffered only one jolt during my time at VTC; it was short—but interesting while it lasted. I was sitting in class one day when our director walked in, flush-faced and nervously playing with his hands. "Mr. Tolle, please come with me," he said, and I did. He took me to an unused classroom, where three men sat at a large table, an empty chair directly across from them. I had no trouble identifying where I should sit and just as quickly guessed that from their stern demeanor, dark suits, white shirts, and narrow ties that they were FBI agents. I was right. It seems that after I had left #1681 35th Street to live with Barbara, some unrequested mail addressed to me had continued to arrive. On one such—an invitation to join a book club—some wit had decided to write, "I will kill President Nixon on [date]" and had then mailed it in. I was asked to write the same words on a piece of paper, and a brief perusal by each agent quickly satisfied them that I had not written the threat. They thanked me, I went back to my class, and that was that. I did briefly wonder how many such pieces of crap they had to deal with on a regular basis.

In many ways, this was the best of times. I was newly married and unable to take my work home at night. I made good money watching some of the best acts in show business while 1969–1970 delivered some tumultuous times just outside our window. In other ways, it was the worst of times; it seemed there was always some demonstration or the other going on nearby. I even blundered into some tear gas once, without realizing it until it was too late. It was an experience I hope that few of you ever have, or ever will, share. On December 1, 1969, about halfway through my language training, all questions about my future status with the draft were settled. Previously, when friends asked me my plans, I always replied that I was going to hide from the draft in the last place they would think to look for me. It invariably produced a laugh, but it wasn't a strategy. I rather doubted that USAID service in Viet Nam would be seen as a legitimate substitute for military service there. As the first draft of the Viet Nam Era covered four birth years, it contained 366 dates. The order in which they were drawn determined individual draft status. My birthdate made me number 365. As far as the draft went, I was safe. It was an odd experience. The oddness came from the fact that I was already about halfway through the Vietnam Training Center's one-year language course. So it was not about whether or not I would be going to Viet Nam, but about what I would wear—and do—while I was there.

The "Sideshow" Begins

In March 1970 an event took place that caused me to question the course I was on. The Nixon administration implemented one of the most monumentally stupid foreign policy decisions in 20th century American history. This was to overthrow Prince Sihanouk, the ruler of Cambodia, then undertake military operations in Cambodia itself. The Prince had been insufficiently hostile to the NVA's use of Cambodia's eastern border area for the final stage of the Ho Chi Minh Trail, that much-too-simple title for the complex of roads, paths, and tunnels that originated in the North and by which the insurgency supplied and armed its combat units throughout southern Viet Nam. The NVA had for some time also been using Cambodia's border areas as safe staging and relief zones for its fighters in Viet Nam, greatly angering the U.S.

Prince Sihanouk provided for me the perfect example of then stand-up comedian Woody Allen's famous line, "The lion will lie down with the lamb, but the lamb won't get much sleep." Cambodia was the lamb, with a choice between two lions, North Vietnam and the United States. Lying down with either would be fatal for his country's precarious neutrality, so he attempted to dance between both. He was no Communist, but he knew Cambodia had no army even remotely capable of doing what the Americans were insisting he do, fight the NVA. While he danced and equivocated, the Nixon administration succumbed to that classic American military trait, the need to identify and target the enemy's "command and control" apparatus. We seemed to assume that our adversary must have a structure similar to ours and in the process we created the mythical "Central Operations South Viet Nam" (COSVN), an American-style communications center that supposedly resided just inside Cambodia and directed the insurgency in Viet Nam. We now know that no such command center ever existed, because it wasn't needed. That was not how the NVA conducted the war. It was how we fought, and we assumed everyone else had to also. For this and other less-than-substantial reasons, we convinced ourselves that Cambodia needed a new government, one friendlier to the U.S. and willing to join the war on our side. The result was a coup led by a Cambodian general named Lon Nol, who established his own government and forced Sihanouk to flee. Direct U.S. assault in search of the mythical COSVN followed, a major escalation of the war.

Few leaders in history have matched the cumulative incompetence and corruption with which Lon Nol ruled during his short period in power. The price for America's promotion of this fraud was paid by the Cambodian people, and it would be a heavy one. It would culminate in the genocide of the fanatical Marxist Pol Pot, but it had earlier effects on both Cambodia and the U.S. No one had any way of knowing how horrific the future launched by our invasion would be, but it quickly sparked demonstrations, including the tragic one at Kent State. Most of my civilian colleagues in CORDS XX felt as I did, and we all left as a group to participate in a protest march, which took place without violence. It was, however, much too late to seriously question our plans, so no one quit the program. This was the first time I had to console myself with the fact that my specific purpose in all of this would be to relieve human misery, which appeared to have just been leveraged up a notch. It would not be my last.

There had been so few of us left in CORDS XX that graduation was virtually nonexistent, although there was a final weekend retreat in northern Virginia. As our "graduation" date approached, each of us was told we had achieved an S3/R3 competency in Vietnamese. This was just determined somehow; we did not take anything like a final exam. The designation meant that we had achieved a 3 level on a 0–5 scale in both speaking and writing Vietnamese. This seemed to be their goal, and our instructors professed themselves pleased. I might perhaps have deserved the 3 in speaking, although that would have really depended on the subject under discussion. I did not believe, however, that I deserved the 3 in reading, a feeling shared by those of my classmates I spoke to about this. None of us asked for our rating to be lowered, however.

And then it was all over, in a decidedly anticlimactic manner. We had all shared this small world, and each of us had left with our impressions. But one of my classmates left with the real prize. Co Dep, easily the most beautiful of the instructors, accepted his marriage proposal. He then did the exact opposite of what so many American men had done, and would continue to do; he married a Vietnamese woman and took her *to* Viet Nam. Oddly enough, I never saw him or anybody else from CORDS XX ever again during the two years I would spend in country. I have absolutely no idea what happened to any of them.

In June 1970 Barbara and I flew to Los Angeles to board Pan Am's transpacific flight. On the way, we stopped in Independence, Missouri, and Eureka Springs, Arkansas, to see both sets of grandparents, who, of course, had not met Barbara before. We ended our flight in Manila, where my mother met us at the airport. I thus got the chance to utter that classic line, "Mom, I'd like you to meet your new daughter-in-law." I had been concerned about this. Mom was fully with the plan to have Barbara live with her, but you just never know. As it turned out, my fears were groundless; they got along famously for the six months Barbara spent there. Mom had always wanted a daughter, and better late than never. Leaving Los Angeles, we were again on a 707, and one of the last sights I had out the small window as we taxied to the runway was of a then brand-new 747. As far as new airplane technology went, that would be pretty much it for the next two years. I knew from my time in 1967 that after I reached Saigon it would be pretty much radial engines and tail draggers from then on.

I met the rest of the language students for one week in Taiwan prior to going to Viet Nam itself. This was a series of carefully scripted days visiting farms, listening to farmers extoll their new, small gasoline-powered cultivators and other tools in the process of modernizing the age-old process of growing paddy rice. And drinking hot tea, lots and lots of it. The best part of the week was that we decided to eat each night as a group, going from regional cuisine to regional cuisine. We occupied one large, round table together, night after night. We each made sure to order something different, and everything was placed on a large lazy Susan, which we spun constantly, eating everything in sight. From this I concluded that in the future I would eat anything the Chinese cooked—in China—and that I would not ask what it was.

We weren't too long into our Taiwan visit when we noticed that we were being watched—not by the regular people, although we were something of a sight, but by some well-dressed men, at least one at a time during the evenings when we went out. They always remained in the background, just observing us. We were clearly under surveillance by the government. No one ever confirmed this, of course, but we concluded that it was because one of our group was of Japanese descent. After this week of viewing rural development in a conflict-free setting, we flew to Saigon and our introduction to a rather different type of development work. Except for me, of course. I had no idea where I was going or even what I would be doing. That would change quickly.

THREE

Fighting "The Other War"

Fresh from a week in Taiwan viewing examples of the kind of local development projects that are possible when no one is being shot at, I landed in Saigon in early July. I had brought a suitcase, which accompanied me, and a footlocker, which did not and which I didn't see again until I reached my provincial assignment. This time shuttle buses (with wire mesh over the open windows to keep grenades out) ferried me to my assigned temporary quarters. My previous stop in Saigon during 1967 had been for only one day, and this one was only for two. I didn't get to see much of the city, and what I saw hadn't changed much from before, if at all. That all-encompassing heat was the same, though. This time I didn't stay at the Rex Hotel but at a USAID facility, which was farther away from downtown and quieter.

Using the shuttle that serviced the various city area U.S. government facilities, my first stop the next morning was the building known as USAID I. At the personnel department, I formally processed in, filling out numerous forms to obtain the necessary ID, including a Vietnamese driver's license. Once I left the building, I never entered it again. My connection would always be with another, similar building located not far away, known as "USAID II."[1] My paperwork complete, I was now formally an advisor to the government of the Republic of Viet Nam (GVN), and a soldier in "The Other War."

Virtually every American knows about the war in Viet Nam. It is equally true that almost all of them—excluding, of course, those who were actually there—learned of the war from visual sources: TV cameras back then and a flood of movies (TV specials and YouTube videos more recently). Even the many books and articles published since then are replete with photos. All of them focus on what the vast majority of American soldiers in Viet Nam were doing: fighting the VC/NVA in U.S. military units in the formal way of American war. These units were part of U.S. Army Viet Nam, or USARV. While technically part of the Military Assistance Command Viet Nam (MACV) structure, USARV was, in practice, entirely separate from MACV. Names like Tak To, Au Shau, Camp Carroll, and many others are part of the lexicon of this war; brave men fought and died over them. This was the war Americans saw, with all its explosions, gunfire, smoke, helicopters, and fear. It made for great video, then and now. But there was another war; one that didn't make great TV and which, therefore, was fought almost without notice. There were Americans in Viet Nam fighting this other war before President Johnson committed U.S. combat troops, and some continued to fight it after President Nixon had withdrawn all U.S. forces. Their war is much less known, and the fact that many of those people were civilians is almost totally unknown. I was a participant—and a civilian—in this other war, from mid–1970 to mid–1972. By that time, the war in Viet Nam—the one in which America was involved—had been underway for over a decade, and the lack of success had caused considerable controversy throughout the American establishment in Viet Nam, not to mention Washington, D.C., and America at large. How the war was fought had evolved, and by the time I arrived that evolution had taken its final form.

"Pacification" and CORDS

The United States had initially advised the military and civilian components of the GVN from separate military and civilian staffs—MACV and USAID. The USAID had operated its traditional economic development and stabilization programs, while MACV dedicated itself to winning the war. Everyone realized, in theory, that development required "security," so winning the war required a military focus, or so it seemed. Just how to go about "winning" the war had been controversial from the very beginning, and the controversy did not abate during the entire period of American involvement. Traditional military actions by traditionally structured military units was the American experience, and that was what we tried after General William Westmoreland became commanding officer of Military Assistance Command, Vietnam (COMUSMACV), in 1964. Westmoreland emphasized large-scale "search and destroy" tactics, which killed a great many of the enemy but fewer than the enemy was able to recruit.

By 1966, despite a determined application of this policy of attrition, vast areas of the country were as insecure as they had been years earlier.

Another strategy had been advocated but not accepted by MACV. The Marines, under the different inspiration of their commander, General Lew Walt, had followed what was known as the "oil spot" approach, regularly engaging in local "civic action" projects with nearby villagers. Civic Action emphasized direct U.S. Marine/Vietnamese contact. It placed U.S. Marines in "Combined Action Platoons," living in villages together with local Popular Force units (semi-trained and semi-equipped local villagers who were to protect their neighbors). They would even go out on ambushes together during the night. The results of these were mixed, as a great many of the local PF members desired accommodation, not confrontation, with their relatives and neighbors in the VC. The goal of a Combined Action Platoon was—as it informally was for everyone in the American effort—to "work themselves out of a job." Few CAP efforts succeeded in this task.

The Marines' "Civic Action Program" might forge a close relationship between Vietnamese and Americans, but it virtually ignored the GVN. As a consequence, while it improved the opinion of the local people about the U.S. Marines, it did nothing to improve their opinion of their own government and provided no incentive for their government to improve itself. Therein lay its weakness. Inherent in the Marines' approach of ignoring the local GVN officials had been the assumption that a pacified people would support their government out of gratitude. Unfortunately, the GVN as constituted did not deserve the gratitude of its people. Emerging out of this extended disagreement was a third option, called "pacification." It took a while to emerge as official policy, but once President Johnson embraced the concept it rose to the fore. It more closely resembled the Marine small-unit approach but was built around involving the GVN, thus earning it the support of its people. The first half of the Pacification program involved establishing "security." Separating the people from the guerrillas was the task of the ARVN, advised by their MACV counterparts. Once the people were separated—or, more often, while the struggle to separate them was going on—came the second half of the program: how to actually secure the loyalty of the people. Melding these two efforts—basically military and civilian—together constituted "Pacification," or "The Other War." The greatest virtue of this strategy was that it did not require U.S. combat units, only advisory personnel. This became important as domestic pressure rose to bring the boys home, and it fit in well with a U.S. combat withdrawal. Both "Pacification" and "Vietnamization" can be broadly understood as describing the same process.

The dual—and interlocking—nature of the Pacification effort meant that both the military and civilian aid programs had to be developed and enacted together. To achieve this, a unique change in the U.S. advisory structure took place, one with little precedent and no successors. MACV integrated the military and civilian staffs at every administrative level outside Saigon itself. The goal was "unifying the military and civilian components of the pacification program," and the result was known by the acronym CORDS, which officially came into being in May 1967 as "Civil Operations Revolutionary Development Support." Most existing civilian programs were shifted to CORDS: New Life Development, Refugees, National Police, Chieu Hoi (welcoming VC/NVA defectors), as well as the RD Cadre program and the Village Self Development Program—the core of the whole concept we were to implement. Then there was the Phoenix [Phuong Hoang] Program, run by the CIA, of course. The refugee work I would be doing was ancillary to, and somewhat outside of, the overall development structure, but it was undertaken by provincial GVN employees, so refugee advisors were part of CORDS. The USAID continued to run its standard variety of national development programs, most significantly Economic Stabilization. Virtually all its personnel operated at the national level, living in Saigon and working at USAID I. The USAID also handled land reform and contracted for the necessary technical expertise to do the surveying and questioning on the ground.

The CORDS structure was a separate chain of command from the MACV advisors with ARVN military units, although both reported directly to COMUSMACV. At the inception of CORDS, Robert Komer became General Westmoreland's deputy for pacification, or DEPCORDS. Komer, his successor William Colby (later head of the CIA), and the entire CORDS structure remained outside the military chain of command but were connected to it at the highest level. Each MACV/CORDS advisory team was a mixture of military and civilian personnel at every level, from Saigon down to the individual districts. The goal was a single, integrated chain of command and a single manager at each level, either military or civilian, as the situation seemed to require. Such integration even extended to an individual's job ratings, in civilian terms the Personnel Evaluation Report, or PER. Civilians rated the military under them, and military officers rated civilians, even FSOs. This was a frequent bone of contention, although not in my case, fortunately.

There was a strict adherence to rank and protocol within the American effort, at least whenever that was possible. There was also a fixed comparison of civilian to military ranks. An FSR/8, the lowest USAID level, was equivalent to a second lieutenant, the lowest possible rank of an officer. The comparison proceeded upward; a 7 was equivalent to a first lieutenant, a 6 to a captain, and so on. That made my father, as an FSR/-3, the equivalent of a colonel. The essential point in all this reorganization was that the end product clearly emulated the structure of the government it was advising. It duplicated the structure of the GVN at the national, regional, provincial and district levels, which in practice meant CORDS emulated the GVN in achieving military domination as well, effectively placing the civilian effort under direct military control at every level.

The GVN/ARVN

The military domination of the GVN by the ARVN was obvious in just about every way, beginning with how the countryside was subdivided and governed. The Republic of Viet Nam was divided into forty-four provinces, plus six autonomous cities. These, in turn, were grouped into four regions, often MR (Military Region), but more often referred to as "Corps," i.e., I Corps (pronounced "Eye Corps"), II Corps, III Corps and IV Corps, proceeding north to south. The regional headquarters were, respectively, at Da Nang, Nha Trang, Bien Hoa and Can Tho.

I Corps encompassed only five provinces, but its location just below the DMZ made it a traditional source of enemy activity. By 1970 the name of its northernmost province—Quang Tri—was known to many Americans, usually for tragic reasons. Although geographically the largest of the four regions, II Corps had by far the smallest population. An estimated three million people lived in its twelve provinces, but only about 500,000 of them in the highlands that dominated its area. While the highlands constituted the majority of the territory of the provinces of both I and II Corps, the coastal provinces also possessed a thin strip of flat land between the mountains and the ocean that was suitable for traditional paddy field rice. These areas were far more populated, with the vast majority of the people living along that coastal strip. Partially due to its existing as the donut around Saigon's hole, III Corps was something of an anomaly, Its provinces varied greatly in terrain, from coastal flat areas to the highlands. The Mekong Delta was IV Corps—flat, divided into countless rice fields, and the traditional image of Viet Nam for everyone who learned of it through television.

By the time of my arrival in 1970, the Republic of Viet Nam had an elected "civilian" government, but that was just a cover. The Vietnamese armed forces thoroughly dominated the Government of Viet Nam at every level. Both its president and vice president—Nguyen van Thieu and Nguyen cao Ky respectively—were generals. Thieu had gathered almost total control in his hands (banishing Ky to the sidelines and irrelevance), and his inner circle was entirely military. Given the quality of those in his inner circle, the unfortunate consequences of total military control cannot be overstated. The military extended its domination all the way down the governmental structure, exerting control at every level. Each corps was commanded by an ARVN major or lieutenant general who controlled the ARVN units in his region. Every GVN province chief, in my experience, was also an ARVN officer, usually a colonel. There may have been a few exceptions in the more secure delta area, although I never encountered one. Each province was divided into two or more districts, and again every district chief I met was a military man. I did hear that in the delta civilian district chiefs were more common, but nationally the military clearly dominated.

The ARVN commanders in each region had broad powers and autonomy akin to medieval lords. Their focus was almost entirely military. The degree of the regional commander's involvement with that their civilian staff at the regional level varied with the commander's interest in such things. Province chiefs were ARVN officers but did not command ARVN regular units. They did control the quasi-military organizations within the province, the Regional Forces (RF), recruited within a province and usually kept there, and the Popular Forces (PF), recruited from within a district and usually kept there. The combat effectiveness of these units can be inferred from the fact that we Americans referred to them as "Ruff-Puffs." More relevant to the provincial CORDS staff was the fact that the province chief also commanded the GVN civilian ministry officials assigned to his province, and his word was law.

Duplicating this structure, a MACV/CORDS team existed in every province. Each was headed by a province senior advisor (PSA). They were most often military personnel and held the rank of colonel. A few provinces had civilian PSAs, and I did a temporary duty time (TDY) with one of them, to be discussed later. Each PSA had a deputy, the DPSA. If the PSA was military, then his DPSA was a civilian and vice versa. The rest of the provincial advisory team varied in numbers and composition according to the local situation. Each province was divided into two or more districts and GVN/ ARVN operated teams down to this level. Thus, CORDS created district teams also, again with military usually assigned the district senior advisor (DSA) position. This mandated a civilian deputy DSA (DDSA), but those were always in short supply. All of the young civilians in CORDS XX (except me), for example, were scheduled to be DDSAs. The largest number of civilian CORDS personnel could be found in III and IV Corps. The shaky security situation in I and II Corps (as well as the lack of much of a civilian population in II Corps highland provinces) kept their team numbers lower. The delta, IV Corps, had very few U.S. combat formations and possessed the largest proportion of civilians to military within the CORDS structure because IV Corps was by far the most populated of the four.

When I was in Viet Nam in 1967 CORDS had just been created. "Revolutionary development" was the buzz phrase, a component of the high-priority effort to shift from large-unit warfare to pacification. The Revolutionary Development (RD) Cadre was, in turn, the central component of the program. These were teams of young men recruited and trained to work at the village level in support of self-development programs. They were dressed in black pajamas in direct emulation of the adversary, given weapons (not current models), and often lived in defended compounds, which were intended for village self-defense, not combat in any real sense. Their effectiveness varied greatly, and no easy summation of the program is possible. None will be attempted here. What is significant is that by the time I returned in 1970, the "revolutionary" in the acronym had been replaced by the decidedly less rousing "rural." This was a change of considerable significance. It symbolized the progress most Americans believed had been achieved. GVN efforts were reaching out to villages previously neglected and clearly bringing more of the population under its control. The emphasis was shifting from security—which had largely been attained, or so some thought—to development, hence the change of name if not of acronym. This "achievement" was highly touted, but the principal reason for its success was the slaughter of indigenous VC cadres during Tet of 68. The GVN was pushing out into a semi-vacuum.

Co Van My: The American Advisor

The key to the CORDS structure and method of operation was that every member was only an "advisor." The primary goal of every CORDS officer involved in pacification was to make the GVN/ARVN more responsible, responsive, and honest. We were not to ignore but actively involve the GVN; we were each to become the "counterpart" of a GVN official and "advise" them how to achieve our goals for them (I say "our goals" to make clear that the GVN never fully accepted that our goals were their goals). This meant, of course, that we had no actual authority. A great deal thus depended on what type of relationship we were able to establish with our counterparts.

The underlying purpose of unifying the advisory effort was to exert stronger pressure on the recalcitrant GVN government structure at every level. The GVN had managed to combine the worst elements of its two previous governing systems, the mandarin system and the French system. Both were complex bureaucracies that required that regulations be followed strictly. The sedate pace and obsession with formalities of both systems were more important than results achieved. Both required obsequiousness on the part of those lower in the command structure and provided virtually no means of going around some obstacle, wherever in the bureaucracy it might be located. U.S. advisors at both the district and provincial levels were always inquiring of their counterparts about the status of some request to higher-ups for something, ranging from permission to proceed on some program to the delivery of physical items. The answer was almost always, "I don't know. I have not been told." To any subordinate member of any GVN organization, this was blanket permission to do nothing, because it had always been that way.

A unified CORDS structure provided a means for the reluctant official—or, more likely, his advisor—to get around this problem. If a ministerial official at the provincial level was being obstructed by, say, the province chief, all he had to do was tell his advisor about the problem. The advisor would then report this problem to his superior, usually directly to the PSA at a weekly staff meeting. The PSA would then go to the Province Chief and put pressure on him to solve the problem. If the problem lay at the national level, then the provincial advisor would contact the proper U.S. individual at the regional level, who would then contact the Saigon office, who would in turn go to their counterparts to find out why something wasn't happening. "Advisory pressure" would be applied when the point of blockage was located, and then the problem was solved. Or so it was supposed to be. The unified chain of command on the American side certainly helped, but the Saigon bureaucracy was an obdurate foe. I can testify to that.

"Goodies"

Officially, the job of a CORDS civilian advisor was to do just that, advise. We CORDS officers, at every level, had no authority in the counterpart relationship we were to establish. That was the official line, but the reality, of course, was rather different. "Advisory pressure" could take many forms. The ability of CORDS to pull an end run on the GVN bureaucracy was our major weapon, one of two. The other was a direct appeal to the collective cupidity of the GVN itself. Americans retained control (in varying degrees) of many of the relief commodities ("goodies") the GVN was anxious to obtain. We had mixed motives in sending some of these goodies, but always dominant among them was the simple desire to help people, feed them, house them, whatever. GVN officials, however, looked upon virtually every program—indeed the whole American effort—as an opportunity for personal enrichment.

In truth, the primary function of a CORDS civilian advisor was not to advise; our real job was to deliver these goodies. Specifically, that meant trying to get as much of the goodies as possible to our subject peoples (in my case, refugees), because each amount sent was subject to attrition from those Vietnamese officials to whom we had entrusted the goodies in the first place. Our classes at VTC with ex-advisors had given us ample warning of this problem. Most during their tours in country had come to view "goodies" as a weapon.

"Goodies" was a generic term with many components. As a refugee advisor, the major goody at my disposal would turn out to be "roofing sheets," about which more later. Throughout Viet Nam, however, "Food for Peace" led the goodies list. Food for Peace was a U.S. Department of Agriculture program, also known as P.L. (Public Law) 480, under which various farm products were shipped overseas to relieve areas suffering from famine or those in conflict. These commodities became a familiar sight throughout the "developing world," as it was then called, usually distributed by U.S. government organizations, primarily USAID. Some of the aid was given to voluntary and religious relief organizations in Viet Nam, including the WRC, as I had discovered in 1967.

There were three products available under the Food for Peace program in Viet Nam: bulgur wheat, vegetable oil, and a mixture known as CSM. This was actually a result of a major program change in 1966. Since the law's enactment in 1954, whole commodities, i.e., wheat, other feed grains, and nonfat milk, had been provided to the recipients. After 1966, it became a fundamental part of the program to craft and distribute more nutritional blends of different products instead of just shipping out the commodities themselves. CSM, for example, was (and remains) a powder that contained cornmeal and soy flour (precooked and defatted, respectively), nonfat dry milk, soybean oil, ten vitamins, and six minerals. It came bagged and required cooking for human consumption, although much research had been expended in making it cook as quickly as possible. The other major product, bulgur wheat, was also "fortified" and required cooking.

I had no idea why these particular products had been chosen for the program, but there appears to have been astonishingly little cultural awareness involved in the decision, at least as it came to East Asia. Varieties of corn (technically "maize") and wheat were staples in many parts of the globe, but not in Viet Nam. This was a rice culture from soup to dessert. The French had introduced wheat, and bread had become a part of the Vietnamese diet, but certainly not bulgur wheat nor maize in any variety. Our intentions may have been good, but the program's engineers and developers did not take into account the local people's potential resistance to doing what outsiders said was good for them. Despite all the education about how CSM provided better nutrition for babies and young children, despite the all-too-frequent want of food of any sort, cultural resistance remained high. In Viet Nam neither CSM nor bulgur wheat were ever considered edible, at least by people. These products had some value as pig food, and thus could be found in any local market—black or not—at reasonable prices. We who distributed these commodities knew where the solids were going to end up but distributed them anyway; it was part of the job.

The third product, vegetable oil, was the exact opposite. No one would eat either bulgur wheat or CSM, but everybody needed oil to cook with. It was hugely valuable and thus commanded a high price in the local markets. Its value also made it the subject of some of the greatest ingenuity ever applied to theft. Pallets of oil, as tall as they were wide in an array of tightly packed one-gallon cans wrapped in plastic, tended to arrive at their destinations with the outer layer of cans utterly empty. Close examination would reveal the small hole(s) made by nails or even wire through which the oil had been extracted ever so slowly. The ingenuity behind this theft was matched by patience, for once a pallet of oil went into storage, even the inner cans in the stack would begin to mysteriously become drained. It usually left through only a small hole, and dripped slowly down, over the cans below it (already drained of oil), with some loss, but eventually it would reach the bottom of the pallet, where it would be collected in small and unnoticed containers. The game of cat-and-mouse between U.S. warehouse supervisors and a plethora of inventive Vietnamese, particularly at the local level where the products came to be stored before distribution, often became complex, in the same manner as the Claymore mine struggle we had learned of at Fort Bragg. No matter how hard we tried, a considerable portion of the cooking oil—sometimes a majority, and on occasion all of it—somehow managed to just disappear before its final distribution. This kind of theft took time, and there was some risk involved, although any large warehouse had a semi-organized system of such withdrawals, with a share of the profits spread among the warehouse staff who had helped, even if only by doing nothing, including reporting the problem. We always checked the weight of every can of oil we were about to distribute in order to avoid an embarrassing moment later in the front of villagers.

Despite the universally understood lack of a human market for two of the three products, virtually every Vietnamese authority, whether secular or religious, greatly desired PL 480 commodities. There was money to be made somewhere, because the Vietnamese managed to utilize just about every scrap of what we Americans had considered to be junk, if not garbage, and had thrown away. There was always a market for commodities, regardless of whom or what actually consumed them.

These were some of the realities I would have to deal with in my provincial assignment and some of the weapons I possessed to make the fight. I had learned about most of this from our American ex-advisor instructors at VTC, at least in theory. Now it was time for the actual experience.

FOUR

Bao Loc
July 1970–July 1971

My initial orientation should have included some time in Saigon at the War Victims Directorate (WVD) getting an overall assessment of the refugee situation and my place in it, but that didn't happen. The WVD director was away, and I was greeted by the deputy director, Norman Hearns. He in turn introduced me to the chief of the Refugee Division, Roy Fontall. Roy wasted no time in telling me that I was being assigned to Lam Dong Province in II Corps, where a big refugee resettlement program was about to get underway. Time was short, and I would fly there quickly, without the usual Saigon orientation. My first thought (to myself) was, *"Where?"* I thought I knew something about II Corps, having flown to a number of its provinces, but the name Lam Dong drew a blank. It turned out there were good reasons for this, and, in time, I would come to appreciate them.

My flights from Saigon to Lam Dong Province were my true introduction to Air America's scheduled regional shuttle system. Lam Dong was the southernmost province in II Corps and actually rather close to Saigon, about 100 miles, as the crow flies. But a journey by plane between those two places had to go through II Corps headquarters at Nha Trang, considerably farther away from Saigon than Lam Dong itself. After my flight to Nha Trang, I still had to take a shuttle flight to Lam Dong, and that required an overnight stay, as the regional shuttle left before the flight from Saigon arrived. There were three such shuttle flights out of Nha Trang due to the size of II Corps, and each presented the same problem to passengers from Saigon. This required overnight began my accumulating negative feelings about Nha Trang, which actually was a rather nice small city. My first stop in Nha Trang was brief due to the urgency of getting me to my province, but I did get to meet the War Victims Nha

Trang regional staff. Its chief was Mike McClellan, a tall, hulking man whose demeanor was much more gentle than his appearance. His deputy was Hugh Stans, a much shorter man whose girth had nevertheless earned him the nickname "Huge." It wasn't until later that I developed my feelings toward Nha Trang as regional center, and these men had nothing to do with it. I always respected them both.

One reason I grew to dislike Nha Trang had nothing to do with the town itself but with the fact that I had to fly out of it to get to Lam Dong. The flight out of Nha Trang, a C-47, stopped at two other province head-quarters before Bao Loc, the capital of Lam Dong Province. Phan Rang was okay, as it was a U.S.-built base, large and spacious, with a substantial runway system. Phan Thiet, however, was none of those things. The approach required a descent over the South China Sea to a tiny asphalt strip that began at the edge of a cliff and terminated in hills beyond that were much too close. A pilot mistake on the approach could have abruptly fatal consequences, and the takeoff required you to believe that your plane would be well airborne before the runway ended at the cliff. I thought I had become inured to flying on Air America, but the approach to Phan Thiet awakened old anxieties. After that, the approach to Lam Dong's provincial capital, Bao Loc, featured no obstacles and was a quite welcome bore to fly into. It was a simple airstrip carved out of the jungle (or, more likely, a tea plantation), with no physical obstacles nearby.

I was met upon my arrival by Jim Chrysler, a stocky African American who was the DPSA and thus would be my boss. He loaded me and my suitcase into his Scout and gave me a quick get-acquainted tour of my new home. It didn't take long. The town of Bao Loc was absurdly small and sparsely populated, in truth a mere outline of a town, built largely on a hillside on the south side of QL 20. It possessed a street grid but few buildings, which were unevenly spaced on it. The streets had been graded and small stones poured over them then rolled into a somewhat compact mass. Bao Loc had one—and only one—reason for existence: the highway, QL (Quoc Lo) 20, which ran between Saigon up into the highlands to Dalat. The Bao Loc lay astride QL 20 at approximately the middle of the province, which made it about halfway through the Saigon/Dalat journey itself. Such commercial activity as Bao Loc possessed was grouped along the road and mainly dedicated to servicing travellers between the two cities. Bao Loc had a small version of the standard open-air market—open-sided, with a concrete floor and a roof.

Lam Dong always had been a quiet backwater in the war. The '68 Tet Offensive saw 36 of SVN's 44 provincial capitals attacked. Bao Loc was not one of them. Things would remain that way during my time there. QL 20 was the only paved road in the province. Once you left it, it was red clay all the way. The best-surfaced (some small rock amidst the clay) road in town left QL 20 and proceeded roughly south up a not-too-steep hill. The province HQ was toward the top, and the road then led to the airstrip, which was on the highest ground of all. The strip and a small plane parking area were also asphalt. A small tin shack and the requisite sandbag bunker completed the picture. No Americans actually lived there. Small side streets led off the lower end of the road up the hill from QL 20 to the province HQ, all of them just gravel pressed into the red clay. Along them at intervals sat a few houses of some size and quality on lots laid out with the streets. There were more weed-choked empty lots than buildings.

There was a standard CORDS compound of prefab buildings within a chain link fence in town, but for some reason I was to inhabit a house on my own. I did not object; the house was spacious, far beyond the needs of a single person. There were three bedrooms, but only mine actually had a bed, which was quite nice: king size with mosquito netting strung above and down each side between the posts at each corner. There was only one bathroom, and it had the expected bare minimum equipment, with a floor-level tile shower. As I would be only sleeping there, the lack of furniture and household tools was not an issue, even after my footlocker arrived and I set up my new home.

MACV Advisory Team #38

By being assigned as a refugee advisor to the Ministry of Social Welfare's representative in Bao Loc, I also thereby became a member of MACV Advisory Team #38. The compound for the team's military members lay a short distance east of town, just off QL 20. It housed all the MACV military personnel, both advisors and the more numerous support personnel. It encompassed some previously existing buildings, white with curiously curved red roofs, plus more recent additions. The compound had tall chain-link fencing ("B-40 wire"), coils of barbed wire surrounding it, and bunkers around the perimeter. The entrance was gated and had to be opened for each vehicle entering or leaving. I presumed it had Claymores, but I did not inquire. It also had a clear field of fire for a full 360 degrees, which I would discover was a rarity in Viet Nam.

By Viet Nam standards, Advisory Team #38 was small. It remained relatively stationary in numbers while I was there but was further downgraded shortly thereafter. The total number of military men actually performing MACV advisory functions with a counterpart never exceeded ten, all officers. Only the PSA had attended a training course. His subordinates, two majors and a varying but small number of captains and lieutenants, were on the standard one-year military tour and were given advisory tasks upon arrival. Only one, Major Brown (who was African American), had served as an advisor in-country previously. Then, about two months after my arrival, the new DSA for Bao Loc District arrived, Major Stef Rowski. He was a solid, competent veteran of previous service in country and held the NVA in high regard. He remained the DSA during the rest of my time in Bao Loc, and as almost all of my work was local we saw each other frequently.

There may have been no more than ten MACV advisors on the team, but the support personnel required to maintain them in province was substantial. The U.S. army carries a long logistical tail, and in Viet Nam it was always hugely larger than the body of fighting/advising men. The compound accommodated the few officers and much greater number of enlisted men of the team (with separate messes), plus the crews and support personnel for two Huey gunships that were stationed at the airstrip. I never got a count of people, and the number was changing almost constantly. The team also contained "Romy," a Filipino Third Country National (TCN), whose smiling, friendly personality was a team constant. He was one of a great many such people, usually Filipino or Korean, with mechanical or other abilities, who were employed to perform the more skilled support tasks. While many just serviced generators or other equipment, Romy's job with MACV Advisory Team #38 was to work with local community groups in development programs, mostly VSD. He made himself useful in a number of other ways also.

Lam Dong had only two districts, Bao Loc and Di Linh. Bao Loc was the provincial headquarters, but it possessed a separate small district headquarters located just a short distance from both the town and the MACV compound. The district chief—an ARVN captain—and his PF force lived there. In contrast to the MACV compound nearby it appeared that an enemy could get pretty close before being seen by anybody who happened to be looking. It had virtually no cleared field of fire. Given the short distance between it and the provincial MACV compound, and the fact that Advisory Team #38 was not very large to begin with, meant that the American DSA and his small staff lived in the provincial MACV compound.

For virtually every young CORDS language officer at the provincial or district level, the acid test was how he would function in what was, for all intents and purposes, a military environment. This usually turned on his relationship with the military PSA. That experience varied greatly, and I would later hear some horror stories. However, mine was on the whole quite positive. On the morning after my arrival in the province, I was introduced to the PSA, Colonel Lawrence Thompson, a tall, ramrod-straight man with close-cropped grey hair. He was polite but correct, a manner he would retain throughout our entire time together. Colonel Thompson was a straight arrow, and he ran things formally, in the army way, which required considerable adaption on my part. He delivered some lessons on the limits of how much a subordinate could say to his superior but without any attitude about my being a civilian. I, in turn, immediately realized the nature of the environment I was in and resolved to behave in the correct manner, at least as far as possible.

As Jim, the DPSA, drove me around for my get-acquainted tour, he mentioned that although he was now a civilian he was also an ex-Green Beret. This did not square with his appearance or his demeanor. He had acquired considerable weight and always presented an easy-going, relaxed personality, smiling frequently. His physical changes were explained when he said he lived in a private house nearby with his Vietnamese wife. He, the police advisor (whom I would meet a short time later and who lived in the CORDS compound), and I were the only civilians on the team. I met the police advisor, Fred Gymball, that evening in the officers' club. He was of medium height, mid–50s in age, and sturdily built, with something of a bulldog look. As we were introducing ourselves I noticed his wedding ring and asked if he had brought his family to a safe haven. No, he said, he had moved them to Australia. He hated the liberal crap that had "taken over the country," and neither he nor his family was ever going back. That was when I decided I was the only civilian on Advisory Team 38.

The Highlands

I was now in Viet Nam but in an environment far different from the stereotypical view of Viet Nam among the American public, i.e., a flat land covered in rice paddies. That was the Mekong Delta, south of Saigon, but I was now about sixty miles north of Saigon, at the southern end of what was broadly known as the Central Highlands. The contrasts were striking. The highlands were sparsely populated and almost entirely forested, in stark contrast to the heavily populated and intensively cultivated lowlands. The highlands produced dry-field rice but was more prized for its natural resources. Its climate was a marked contrast to that in the lowlands, and the French had founded numerous plantations growing such things as tea and had turned the small town of DaLat into a vacation resort.

Regardless of province and the specifics of geography (some provinces are more mountainous than others), the soil of the highlands was all the same: red laterite clay. The rainy season turned it into a glutinous mess, annoying to those properly equipped but rather more than that to U.S. civilian advisors, as I would soon learn. The dry season held less peril but more consistently produced a red dust that was virtually everywhere and easily stirred up. Helicopters were the worst, of course, and any motor vehicle driven off-road could lay quite a trail. Just walking would do a decent job also. It was hard to say what I liked better about the highlands, the scenery or the climate. The hills at all points along the horizon were simply beautiful, a lush green. Along either side of QL 20 that green tended to be more orderly, in the form of tea plants. The mist among the hills in the early morning was a marvelous sight. That mist was due to the fact that in the highlands the temperature dropped overnight to the dew point and below. The days could be hot, but nothing compared to that of Saigon. And when the sun went down, so did the temperature. I had brought along in my footlocker a windbreaker, for no reason that I can remember. It turned out to be a very good thing to have, as my work required me to depart my house early in the morning and my leisure activities meant I returned to it late at night. As I would drive out in the morning past the already fully awake central market area, the sight of Vietnamese women wearing sweaters or jackets always brought a smile to my face. It was so incongruous compared to anywhere in the lowlands.

The highlands produced a variety of products, mostly from its forests, but Lam Dong's product was tea. Extensive plantations occupied most of the suitable land along both sides of QL 20, and some extended outwards a good distance. We all assumed that the owners—Frenchmen who had married local women—had some sort of agreement with the other side. The French and the Americans did not socialize. The Vietnamese controlled every activity in the highlands, including every business of any size at all. Fully half of the population in the area were not Vietnamese at all but belonged to one of several hill tribes, most of ancient Malay extraction. These people had been, up until the arrival of the French, barely living in the iron age. The French called them Montagnards, or "mountain people." The Vietnamese called them *moi*, or "savages," and treated them with a policy that encompassed a spectrum from disdain to persecution. It was during my time in the Central Highlands that I began to consider the possibility that it was racism that made the world go round.

The Vietnamese despised the Montagnards, but the Americans had what amounts to a love affair with these people, calling them "Yards" and meaning it with affection. I personally heard several grizzled army veterans proclaim how much they loved the Yards. The hill tribes of Southeast Asia bought into the promises of the Americans to a remarkable extent and proved to be our best native allies during the war, staffing some of the most hazardous Green Beret camps deep in hostile territory and suffering considerable casualties as a result. But they had no love for the GVN and reportedly manned some of the enemy's forces in the region. If so, while they may have manned these formations I am sure they didn't command them. The Vietnamese were Vietnamese, after all. But the bottom line was that the majority of the Montagnards—assuming such a census could be taken, which it couldn't—wanted only peace. Whoever won, they would still be persecuted. The real reason virtually every American who encountered the Montagnards loved them was that they were trustworthy; they did not steal. If an American left pretty much anything unattended near a Vietnamese, it would disappear. Around Montagnards, your possessions were safe. While I am sure that American materialism corrupted a portion of the Yard population, the overwhelming cupidity of the Vietnamese made the Montagnards a special people in American eyes.

The Montagnards of Lam Dong were from the Koho (pronounced *K'Haw*) tribe and every one of them I met through the advisory team had names that began with *K*) My personal bodyguard/interpreter was K'Tom (that's phonetic), a Koho in his late twenties. Most of the team used K'Tom and his fellows as interpreters, as I did initially; but I quickly discovered that his comprehension of Vietnamese exceeded his ability to express it in English. Given that he was interpreting between his second and third languages, I was still impressed. But once I discovered how our Vietnamese treated him and all the Montagnard interpreters (which didn't take long), I brought him along more for potential assistance than interpreting. He proved to be reliable, loyal, and honest. One afternoon I decided for no good reason to drive away from QL 20 along one of the several dirt roads that led to the tea plantations. K'Tom was with me, in the passenger seat of the Scout. He always carried an M-16 rifle but normally kept it down below his knees when we were in my vehicle. On this trip he just sat quietly for the first few minutes, as we remained within cultivated areas that had to be tended frequently. As we drove farther, he brought his rifle up into his lap. As I drove still farther, he rolled down his window, and shortly after that stuck the rifle barrel out. When he turned off the safety, I decided to turn around. When I left the province, K'Tom gave me one of the most cherished souvenirs of the highlands, an engraved copper bracelet. These had traditionally been awarded in ceremonies, but the influx of Americans had cheapened everything, and some even appeared for sale in local markets. I was touched and wore it regularly (despite how it stained my wrist green), until many years later when it was no longer practical to work with it on. After I put it away, I slowly lost track of it and at some point lost it. I regret that greatly.

Refugees

I had received only the barest briefing in Saigon about my upcoming assignment, but I quickly understood the context. The U.S. invasion of Cambodia had returned to haunt me, full time. The refugees I would be assisting were an almost unique group among those many who were described as such at one time or another during this long war.[1] Technically, the overwhelming majority of those so described weren't legally refugees at all, at least according to international law. To become an officially counted "refugee," an individual must flee (from a variable list of threats) *across a national border*. Those Vietnamese fleeing combat to GVN-controlled areas, being relocated or otherwise displaced for a large number of reasons, were technically "war victims," because they did not cross any national border.

But the people whose reception and resettlement in Lam Dong Province I was being sent to facilitate fit the international definition of refugees. They were also victims of war but less directly than most. They were not fleeing combat but ethnic cleansing. The term hadn't come into common use yet, but that is what it came down to. The Vietnamese who were coming my way had been residents of Cambodia, virtually all of them natural-born Cambodian citizens and some having been there for generations. Vietnamese had largely constituted the class of small merchants and businessmen in Phnom Penh, and their relative wealth made them targets. Those plotting against Sihanouk had been exploiting anti-Vietnamese feeling among Cambodians for some time, and the coup provided some of them with an opportunity to achieve economic gain under the guise of patriotism. Both the new government and many of its people saw an opportunity to rid the city of its Vietnamese residents. This was a mixture of ethnic hatred and financial greed, as there was money to be made by evicting those who were, after all, the enemy now. They were being evicted en masse, and the GVN planned to settle 5,000 of them in Lam Dong. They were to begin arriving by the end of the month, or at least that was what I was told in Saigon.

On my first full day in Lam Dong, I introduced myself to Mr. Khiem, the province representative of the GVN Ministry of Social Welfare, who would be my counterpart. He was plump and round-faced for a Vietnamese and wore a moustache. I never asked him his age, as that would not have been polite. He looked to be in his mid–30s, so I guessed mid–40s. He had been doing this job for a few years now, making me acutely conscious that I was only 23 and this was my first real job, yet I was his "advisor," there to suggest how he might do things better. I knew he had had previous American advisors, and I got to thinking about how ridiculous it was to inflict an endless series of new "advisors" on the same GVN official when each of them had to spend so much time just learning the basics of what he was supposed to be improving. This first meeting was a brief one. I had come to see him to show respect and had resolved to severely limit my questions, for good form's sake. I did learn some interesting information, however. What I had been told in Saigon was wrong. Mr. Khiem revealed that we would be receiving 10,000 refugees, not 5,000, and that they would begin arriving within a week. This news severely tested my resolve about not asking questions, but cultural adaptation had to begin from the first moment, so I remained friendly, solicitous, and brief. We would be seeing enough of each other soon. He also mentioned the big meeting of everyone involved in the project that was scheduled for the next day. I had not heard of it and was duly grateful to him.

On my second day in province I stood as inconspicuously as possible to the side of a substantial crowd that had assembled outside the province headquarters for the meeting about the incoming refugees. Everyone present was a GVN employee or worked for some social agency. Actually it was more of a pep rally, but it demonstrated that the refugees were going to be welcomed by the existing population. The province chief started things off with a few words and then introduced the "point man" for the project, Major Thoai. Whatever problem anyone had was to be taken to him. The province chief then left and Major Thoai took over. I had done okay following what the province chief said, as he kept it to simple exhortations. But almost immediately after Major Thoai began speaking, I was lost. I had no idea what he was saying. This came as quite a shock. I had, after all, just spent a full year learning the language, or so I thought. I knew why I was having such a problem, but that didn't promise to make things any easier. I had been schooled entirely by southerners at VTC and had understood the province chief because he was a southerner also. Major Thoai, however, was from the north. His pronunciation of several words was distinctly different, along with the northern dialect being in general harsher in tone. This was going to be a major problem. I also learned to my dismay that the Vietnamese population of Bao Loc, and indeed of Lam Dong itself, were overwhelmingly northerners, so my problem was going to be widespread. That means they had once been refugees themselves, among the 800,000 Vietnamese who fled to the south in 1954 after the French defeat. The vast majority who made the move were Catholics. They had often come as entire villages, at the urging of their local priest. The passage of time had not greatly softened their accents, and this would be a continual source of frustration for me. Communication at the level I had expected was going to be difficult.

The population of Bao Loc did seem to have been mobilized, from RD Cadre teams to groups from the local high school, religious organizations, and even representatives of the larger local businesses (not very large, mind you). Large amounts of materials, from tents to cans of food, had been stockpiled, as the refugees were expected to arrive without much of anything. PL 480 commodities were on hand, and I was even given a small cash fund of piasters to spend should I find it necessary. The refugees would arrive at the Bao Loc airstrip on Air America planes and be met and processed and then taken to the area selected for their resettlement, not far from Bao Loc and down in the valley of a small stream. It was to be named "Nam Phuong." Mr. Khiem and I spent some time totaling up what we had, from both GVN and U.S. sources. The immediate need was tents, food, water, and blankets. A substantial number of both tents and blankets had been laid in, because it gets cold in the highlands at night and these refugees were from much hotter Phnom Penh.

My first visit to the Nam Phuong site confirmed that the initial steps that needed to be taken in advance seemed to have been taken. The site had many large tents assembled into rows, latrines had been dug, and a place had even been laid out for the first central market. We had a considerable number of roofing sheets on hand to use when the permanent homes began to be built. Mr. Khiem also had at his disposal a considerable amount of various other items, shipped by the GVN or locally acquired. Most were food items in cans. It seemed like as much preparation had been made as could have been and that the Vietnamese side was ready. I was less sure of myself.

As Mr. Khiem had predicted, the Air America planes began arriving six days after I had. By that time, I had at least learned how to get from the airstrip to the refugee site, but I was very much still finding my way around. That first day was one of some pageantry, as the refugees were met by just about everyone, organized into their sponsoring groups with banners and ribbons. The province chief ceremonially welcomed the first planeload. The migration took several days to play out as load after load of C-47s and C-46s disgorged their uprooted and disoriented occupants. The pageantry quickly decreased, but every day each planeload was met by a Vietnamese delegation and taken first to a central processing center at old French buildings pressed into service. Once properly registered, they were transported to Nam Phuong, where they were processed further and assigned to a tent. The reception was well run, and the best evidence of that was that I had nothing to do but stand around and look professional.

This was my first opportunity to put into practice something that had bugged me about the actions of some of the Americans in Viet Nam. I was acutely conscious of my foreignness and strongly of the opinion that Americans should not take a prominent role in GVN ceremonies. I believed even more strongly that we Americans should not walk around

As old as a C-47, but much more rare: a Martin C-46, 1970.

with cameras taking photos. Far too many CORDS civilians—and no small number of military men—did just that, snapping away at the sights. I had a camera, a new one in fact, and did take some photos from time to time, but NEVER during any formal ceremony or event. Today, of course, it would be nice to have some photos to back up my memory, but I stand by my belief. Such photos from the period 1970–1972 included in this book are almost always the work of others and were given to me.

By the end of the first day's arrivals, I had noted a few surprising things about "my" refugees. The remaining five days of arrivals confirmed that this group was somewhat different from your average, run-of-the-mill refugee (yes, refugees were so common that we adopted something of a black humor in our shop talk). The in-country refugees all too frequently generated in Viet Nam were overwhelmingly farmers, residents of a countryside that had long been contested but was now in the grip of a destructive ferocity that dwarfed all that had gone before. As such, they tended to arrive almost without belongings, having lost what few possessions they had when forced to flee, often on a moment's notice, if that. Not so my refugees. Some had been farmers, but many others had been middle-class professionals, even entrepreneurs and business owners. As the planes disgorged their occupants day after day, I was frequently astonished at what possessions some of the refugees had been able to bring. One individual arrived with a large, beautiful old prewar AJS motorcycle. I have no idea how he convinced people to help him get that beast on the plane. The furnishings for more than one small restaurant, complete with tables, chairs, and tablecloths, arrived and were quickly set up for business in their new country. I heard that one madam and her stable of prostitutes also arrived and were equally quick in returning to business. The restaurants were obvious, but the existence of the whorehouse was never confirmed. It was none of my business, and I didn't inquire. The final irony was that even though my people were about the only internationally recognized "refugees" they were not given that title. They were officially the "Vietnamese Repatriates" (*Viet Kieu Hoi Hung*). Note the use of the term "repatriates" to obscure the reason for their arrival and the lack of any reference to Cambodia.

On the second day of the airlift, I finally had something to do. A young woman on Mr. Khiem's staff ran up to me with a problem. There were several ad hoc collections of relief commodities to be distributed, and one of them was a sizeable stock of canned fish. As the MSW staff were setting up to distribute the cans, someone discovered that there were no can openers, either on the cans or anywhere else. The young woman suggested that she to go the Bao Loc market area and try to purchase some. There were no MSW funds for such individual circumstances, but that was what my contingency fund was for. Thus armed, she left and came back in not much more than an hour with a large plastic bag containing more than a thousand of the U.S. military's standard field issue P-38s, the small, folding can openers that take up very little space or weight but require some work to actually use. We were thus able to issue one to every three or four families. The fact that several families were grouped together in each of the large tents made this arrangement reasonably practical. I marveled that so many of a common U.S. military item could be obtained in such an out-of-the-way local market in the southern highlands, where the American military had barely made a presence.

The total airlift required six days to accomplish. There were a limited number of Air America C-47s (and fewer of the more commodious C-46s) available for such a sustained effort, so I got used to seeing the same tail numbers arrive and leave. It all proceeded without a hitch; each planeload was met, registered, and delivered to Nam Phuong. So far, so good. About midway through the airlift Stan Anders, from WVD Saigon, formerly assigned in Bao Loc, and who knew Mr. Khiem, arrived to look things over. I appreciated his delaying his visit and not stepping on my toes, if only as a message to the Vietnamese. He pronounced things to be going well and departed shortly, to report to Roy at WVD.

Mr. Khiem and I met frequently, and I made it a point to praise the way things had gone so far. Otherwise, I had little to actually do, because of that fact. I made daily tours of the site in my Scout and began to keep track of the changes that had already begun to take place. Oddly enough, I never got an accurate count of how many refugees had arrived. That was largely because that number kept changing. There were some discrepancies among the initial distribution lists, but I believe the number initially exceeded—by a small margin—the expected 10,000 total. But then it began to drop. Some of the new arrivals left quite quickly, apparently having relatives in country. Most elected to stay, at least for a while. People continued to leave on a steady basis, but by then no one was attempting

The author, Stan Anders and Mr. Khiem observing a refugee interview at Nam Phuong, 1970.

to keep accurate numbers beyond those of individual commodity distributions.

The initial enthusiasm and cooperation among the various groups in and about Bao Loc began to wane rather quickly. The provincial MSW employees under Mr. Khiem soon bore the burden of the work as the other local groups disbanded or went elsewhere. Then again, the presence of such a mobilized force was no longer needed. Things began to stabilize. Once the final distribution of reception items had been made, there was a pause as the individual families made their decisions about their future. Then construction of more permanent homes began. This was the point at which the most popular goodie we refugee advisors possessed, roofing sheets, was dispersed, a fixed number for each new house to be built. The more the new village grew the more it possessed a noticeable ability to reflect sunlight, from walls as well as from roofs.

Nam Phuong was divided into two segments by the small stream that ran through the site. The portion at the site's entrance had been laid out for the reception tents, and alongside its main "road" there grew the initial shops and market area. It was along here that those tables and chairs I had noticed being unloaded appeared as new restaurants. The remainder of the site was across the stream. A pipe had been laid under the road to accommodate the flow of water (or so I was told), but that stretch of road was constantly muddy and thus dangerous for a Scout. It would not be long before I found out just how dangerous.

My work during this period after the initial reception consisted largely of checking in regularly with Mr. Khiem, driving around keeping an eye on the site, and signing my name. The GVN adhered strictly to "the French system," which means "many copies of everything, all of them to be signed by many people." I was one of them, attesting by my signature that this or that product had been distributed to the people on the list. I must have signed my name a thousand times a week, or so it seemed. I suspected that the unending lists actually contributed to why we never came up with a consensus count of just how many people were living in Nam Phoung. That was a problem, because when I was driving around the site I was also counting. Counting was how we measured progress.

I quickly became aware of just how much time I would be spending briefing other people about the resettlement project and that all of them expected numbers in my presentation. This was both bad and good news. Absent the all-important fundamental "total" number, I had to do some verbal tap dancing about how people kept leaving, making an accurate count impossible. This was a weak point in my presentation, for sure. To compensate, I quickly learned that I should keep track of the individual signs of progress in the camp. As refugees moved from tents into new housing, I regularly recorded the declining number of tents still occupied. Likewise, I kept track of and updated constantly the number of homes under construction, the number of them under roof, the number occupied, and so on. The Vietnamese had no need of such information, but I did. Numbers were the sine qua non of that curious ritual in which I found myself performing a lead part, "The Military Briefing."

The Military Briefing

Colonel Thompson had quickly and decisively introduced me to the basic concepts surrounding this ritual during the first staff meeting of which I was a part, soon after my arrival. From him I learned that when it was my turn to speak, I was to be short (they don't call it "briefing" for nothing) and after I had my say to shut up. If the colonel spoke after I did about something I had said it didn't mean he wanted to hear any further from me. We held these conferences on Friday afternoons, and everyone was expected to contribute something about what they had done that week, so I soon learned the drill.

But I really had to up my game once the refugee movement into my province became nationally known, which didn't take long. I knew in advance that I would be hosting several people who wanted me to inform them about what was happening; that was to be expected. Mike McClellan and Hugh Stans from Nha Trang came by and wanted to learn, but we could have a civilian-to-civilian conversation among specialists without much deference to rank. These were all my superiors, but we could discuss things. When the military began to drop in, I found myself doing something quite different. I now had to brief high-ranking officers from all over the country who had no real connection to what was happening and weren't there to offer any help, and I had to do it in the standard military manner. Two-star generals were my most frequent visitors, for reasons I never understood. It may be because that rank gave them their own helicopter. I often saw the task of briefing a general strike fear into the hearts of the junior military members of Team #38, but I undertook it as a learning experience and so it proved to be. It wasn't that difficult, actually, as the format was simple and never changed. Once you learned the rules for addressing your military superiors, you were halfway there. These were few and simple: employ a firm diction, display a positive attitude at all times, try your hardest to avoid negativity—or even uncertainty—and, above all, do not even attempt to introduce nuance.

This was all classic military, of course, but the Viet Nam conflict was a numbers war; it was all about numbers. Absent any defined fronts and facing an opponent that quite sensibly strove to avoid large-scale direct conflict, winning became defined by quantitative measures, from "body count" after combat to "blood trails" leading from Claymore mine ambushes. Civilians had introduced letters in the form of the Hamlet Evaluation System (HES), but the result of "A," "B," "C," or "VC" was determined by numerical inputs. In this manner, numbers substituted for solid, reliable information, which was always in even shorter supply than we assumed.

Whenever some general was to arrive for a briefing, I would drive down to Nam Phuong and go through my counting ritual, updating those all-important numbers. Thus armed, I would step up to give my briefing knowing exactly what was going to happen. I would spend a few minutes crisply spewing out facts about how many refugee buildings had being constructed, how many were under roof, how many were completed and occupied, and so on. Upon completion of my initial pitch, I would ask if there were any questions, then patiently await what I knew was coming: "THE QUESTION." The general would furrow his brow, appear to consult his notes, and then ask … a minor, second-tier question. By "second-tier" I mean that it would never be about any of the major, significant issues at stake. Each general would use THE QUESTION to ignore those, thus implying that he understood those major issues and wanted to demonstrate his grasp of the subject by addressing a minor point on which he still needed some clarification.

These inquiries were thus often unanticipated, which was part of the point, of course. Under the rules of THE MILITARY BRIEFING, when THE QUESTION was asked, I had only two possible options: (1) give the information if I actually possessed it, or (2) if I didn't, recite the following mantra: "I don't have that information, sir, but I will look into it and get back to you as soon as possible." This had to be repeated, word for word, although both the general and I knew that wasn't going to happen. He was shortly going to board his helicopter and leave, probably not giving another thought to Nam Phuong on the flight back or thereafter. I was going to go about my business and not try very hard to contact him with the information.

Somewhat later, after my confidence in my analysis of the situation and its requirements had been bolstered by repetition, I decided to add a third option: making up an answer, i.e., lying. This was pure ego, of course, that of an opinionated young man in an environment where young men listen, say "yes sir," and then do what they are told. I didn't lie to any civilian visitor, because all were in some way connected to the project. Some two-star that just dropped in, had no reason to be there, and would forget every fact and detail immediately after departing yet expected attention and deference while he was here occasionally left with my answer to his version of THE QUESTION made up on the spot, out of whole cloth. They always left satisfied. The highest-ranking official I briefed was a civilian. He was William Colby, then the DEPCORDS, meaning he was the deputy for CORDS to MACV commanding general Creighton Abrams (who had replaced Westmoreland in July 1968). During my tenure "Ambassador" Colby (he was always referred to in that way, although the U.S. ambassador to the Republic of Viet Nam was Ellsworth Bunker) visited Lam Dong Province on a two-pronged visit. One of his tasks was to distribute some of the small, gasoline-powered, walk-behind cultivators to some farmers in a typical GVN ceremony, and the other was to be briefed by me about Nam Phuong.

This was attention from just about the highest quarter. There was also a secondary consideration, a personal one. I have written previously of my father's ability to make friends among the lower-ranking men in country, but he was equally adept in meeting people further up the ladder. One of them was William Colby, and my father had mentioned me to him. This was a potential route to government service after CORDS, and I was determined to make a good impression. Despite that, I had to, in good conscience, tell him that while the reception and initial resettlement phases had been well handled, things had come to a standstill over land distribution. This wasn't the feel-good varnish I had been subtly encouraged to deliver during my military briefings, but it was the truth. It seems that I did make a good impression, despite my less-than-positive summation of the situation and some pre-briefing travails, as I will relate below. It wasn't a formal briefing; Ambassador Colby was a low-key guy. It was all business until the end, when he shook my hand and said he would have good things to say to my father the next time he met him.

The first seven or so months of my time in Bao Loc proved to be active, as the refugees within my purview needed some time to settle in. Despite how relatively well-stocked some of them had been, they were still refugees, expelled from their homes by old neighbors who had suddenly decided to hate them. Some had family in Viet Nam and left the camp to be absorbed into the population elsewhere. A solid majority remained, and after settling in they waited for what was supposed to happen next: the distribution of nearby land, as Nam Phuong was planned to be a permanent community. The number of them with commercial backgrounds would be useful in the community, but land ownership would make or break the project.

It took about seven or so months to establish a reasonably viable, if entirely artificial, community. A central market of sorts had been established, and those who had arrived with the tools of a trade had established such small enterprises in their new country. Galvanized roofing sheets were the material of choice, not only for roofs but for walls as well. This bright display set amidst the red highlands dirt gave a distinctly raw visage to the place. But that's what it was, a still-raw gridded order imposed on what had been open land.

One of the projects at Nam Phuong after the reception phase was the building of a small schoolhouse. This was a refugee project supervised by Mr. Khiem (and thus myself), instead of being a school built under the Village Self Development Program, for which I would have had no responsibility. That meant it was the only such project that I encountered for which I was both forewarned and forearmed and thus understood where potential problems might be. I was ready to actually advise if called upon to do so. This was due to my father's having been an education advisor and having shown me around several small schoolhouses he had supervised being built.

We walked through a few, and he had spoken bitterly of the corruption and deceit that surrounded any project that involved giving money to local contractors, with schools a principal target. There were a number of ways one might shortchange the work to garner some more profit. Usually it involved the concrete that was specified for every floor. Skimping on the amount of cement, the strength of the mix, or the quality of the aggregate was common, but most common of all was to pour the slab too thin. It was usually OK around the perimeter, which could easily be checked, but the middle of each floor was notorious for being thin, often so thin that the footfalls of the students would cause it to crack soon after the school opened.

I thus paid special attention to the first school to be built at Nam Phuong, particularly the concrete work. The project began with one of those small but important ceremonies the Vietnamese loved to enact. This one was called the "Ceremony of Receiving the Rock." With the widespread corruption, a careful check on how much of what commodity that was delivered was very important, and semi-public ceremonies were employed where possible. When cement was delivered, for example, it was no big deal. It came in bags, and there was no point in doing anything beyond counting their number. Aggregate, however, was much easier to cheat on, so Mr. Khiem put on a ceremony to "receive" it. I was asked to observe, of course, and I did. The contractor supplying the aggregate brought it in the back of a truck. He first produced a square-walled form, open on both top and bottom and with beams extended both front and back for carrying. I was told this form could hold one cubic meter when leveled off at the top. Workers placed it on the ground, then filled it once with aggregate, lifted it up, moved it closely nearby, and repeated the process until the proper amount had been ceremonially "received." This was followed by handshakes, bows, and smiles all around, all in front of those refugees who had wondered what was going on and had stopped by.

Houses, markets, and schools were all well and good, but the answer to the issue of long-term viability was land, or rather its ownership. Resolution of that issue did not lie with the Ministry of Social Welfare in Saigon, however. Land titles were to be issued by the Ministry of Land Reform. This would test the CORDS concept of bypassing the GVN bureaucracy, because CORDS was not involved with the Land Reform Program. I began to ask Mr. Khiem about the land question, and he always answered with a shrug. He had done his job, and he had done it well. I did not advise him and his staff how to do a better job, as that had not been necessary. He would continue to be involved with the refugees, but his primary job was reception and temporary resettlement.

Thus did the resettlement project for the Vietnamese Repatriates from Cambodia, after a well-executed reception phase, gradually slip into that all-too-common status in Viet Nam, somewhere between unknown and pending. Thus also did my workload lighten, slowly but steadily. I had always been carrying out other tasks, except during those first few weeks when I was too new to be of any use anyway. Gradually, however, I found the time to be assigned other work. That allows me the opportunity to discuss more of the day-to-day routine of my job, although it was always so full of uncertainty—frequently justified—that use of the word "routine" might be questioned.

As Time Goes By

Because the reason for my presence was so close, I quickly established a daily routine traveling between my house, the site, and the MACV compound. I slept in the nice, overly commodious house I had been provided, but that was about all. The footlocker containing my things finally did arrive, the delay coming because it too had to go through Nha Trang. The things in it didn't fill my closet, let alone a three-bedroom house, furnished though it was. I neither cooked nor ate there, so virtually every hour between early morning and late at night I could be found elsewhere. I was never bothered by mosquitos at Bao Loc's altitude, but I quickly noticed that the house came equipped with a full array of cockroaches. I made the usual attempts to control them with such chemicals as were available, but with no success. I was young then and didn't have to go to the bathroom during the night. That was a good thing.

As I was living alone, I was issued two guns, both vintage World War II, an M1A2 carbine and a type of submachine gun whose circular shape had given it the nickname "grease gun." I took both out to a semi-official range the advisory team had established and tested them. I fired the carbine in single-shot mode, as its mechanism appeared decidedly old and dingy. I determined it would probably work if required. I decided that the grease gun might be useful if I ever wanted to knock down a wall. Its .45 caliber slugs packed quite a wallop. Unfortunately, it jammed every three or four rounds, so even knocking down that wall would have taken some time. I put it away and forgot about it. There was also a small sandbag shelter built on the rear patio abutting the house. I checked it out with a flashlight shortly after my arrival and decided that no one had ever been required to enter it yet. For me to do so, and join the various creatures that seemed to have taken up abode in the darkness, would require some serious motivation. Although Bao Loc was, on occasion, rocketed or mortared, none ever came anywhere close to my quarters, so I never found out exactly what creatures lived in there, although I did spend a few nights watching the show on the horizon. No one had counted on me to protect myself, fortunately. My safety was entrusted to a group of Montagnard guards who occupied the grounds at night. There was a fence around the perimeter of the property and a gated entrance to the spot where I parked my Scout.

I often ate breakfast on the road, as it were. A bakery in Bao Loc produced those small French rolls I would later find in Saigon. They were sold by the side of the road in small bags, each showing by its internal condensation that the bread was not only fresh but still warm. They were delicious, and there was no need for butter or anything else on them. I ate pretty much all my other meals at the MACV compound and usually spent my evening leisure time there also. I would eat at the officer's mess and then spend the rest of the evening in the officer's club close by, a small, one-room structure with an equally small bar that always somehow managed to be well-stocked. This was a routine I repeated almost every evening during my eleven-month stay in Lam Dong, and while the food was quite forgettable the evenings at the officer's club are etched in my memory. The primary reason for this was that each evening the officer's club was host to Fred Gymball, the team's police advisor, whom I met that first evening. He always occupied the commanding seat, along the short arm of the bar's *L* shape. A second seat could have been accommodated there, but Fred always occupied it alone and unchallenged. Even on those rare occasions when Colonel Thompson came in to have a drink (and they could be counted on the fingers of one hand during my time there), he always made a point of deferring to Fred.

Fred didn't just sit at the bar; he held court, and an entertaining court it was. Fred Gymball was just that kind of guy. It wasn't his appearance, although that was formidable enough (he had been, after all, a career cop). Fred dominated the bar through the force of his personality. He was a conservative, through and through. This could include any subject ("People tell me Jimmy Hendrix can make a guitar cry; I don't want a guitar to cry, I want a guitar to play"), but he always found the most takers with social issues and, of course, politics. His gambit usually included the other constant at Team 38's officer's club, "Liars Dice." Fred always played and almost never lost. Liars Dice is a drinking game. Fred not only always kept his head, but he had also mastered the game's psychological aspect. He also had an excellent group to practice on. Following the colonel's example, his subordinates—two majors—were not often in the officer's club. This left the slightly larger number of younger officers—lieutenants and captains—to amuse Fred. After hours, away from the colonel's supervision and with a few drinks in them, the younger officers turned out to be surprisingly liberal. Most seemed to have become officers because they felt they were going to be drafted and decided they would rather go as an officer than as an enlisted man. Fred had no greater pleasure than to bait them, listen to their declarations, then leave them sputtering when he concluded things with one of his outrageous but well-phrased comments. These simply could not be followed up, at least by those men. They would just sputter and then grow silent while Fred serenely sipped his beer. I always refrained from challenging Fred, seeing it as an obviously doomed effort, and simply enjoyed the show.

This meant that more often than not I returned to my house well after dark. The gate was always shut and chained, and one of my Montagnard guards would open it when I showed up. At least that was how it was supposed to work. My guards all had day jobs; consequently, chances were that when I arrived back late in the evening they would all be asleep. Sometimes my headlights served to wake one up, and he would open the gate. Otherwise I had to honk the horn. As I went to bed shortly thereafter, I always consoled myself with the thought that, as my house was located at about the center of town, any attackers would have made some noise before getting close to me. My guards were always gone by the time I woke up in the morning.

I found additional comfort in the fact that just down the street from me was a small, two-story building that had been converted into a U.S. military compound. I was initially taken aback, however, when I first saw by whom. Somehow, here in Bao Loc, up in the hills and many miles from anything remotely resembling a body of water, there was a contingent of the U.S. Navy. They were part of the Military Public Health Advisory Program (MILPHAP), whose job it was to both minister to the considerable basic health needs of the local population and to train locals in the necessary procedures. The team had fortified the building with the usual wire and sandbags and used it for both sleeping and, well, partying. My first visit confirmed what I had begun to believe after hanging around the navy men at the Da Nang tech school in '67, that the U.S. Navy believes in living well. That little group lacked for nothing and actually managed their own mess, despite being no more than ten in number. I ate there only occasionally, although their food was clearly superior. A representative of the team did usually attend the Friday briefings, but otherwise I saw little of them, at least until the Christmas holidays rolled around. Then it was different. They knew how to party.

As a civilian, I was assigned a personal vehicle. It was equipped with a military radio, and I was given a call sign. Anyone driving about anywhere in the province was expected to use it, primarily to report to the Tactical Operations Center (TOC) both their departure from and their later arrival back at Bao Loc. The military personnel on the team adhered to this (of course), but I was rather lax. I spent a lot of time driving around from one place to another but always near Bao Loc. I felt that reporting all this was totally irrelevant to the TOC. When I drove a longer distance, to B'Sar to the south or to Lam Dong's other district, Di Linh, I would report in, but it was some time before I drove to either location.

Getting Around on the Ground

One of the things I learned immediately upon arrival in Lam Dong was that the security situation did not seem to have improved since I was last in country in 1967. It was remarkable just how little of the Vietnamese countryside was actually "secure," i.e., controlled by our side, even in so quiet a province as Lam Dong. American civilians drove vehicles only within their immediate area. Whatever the location or circumstance, all journeys by road were day trips, and the phrase meant exactly that; all trips had to be completed within the passage of one day's sunlight. American civilians never went out after dark. This was not to say that the VC/NVA roamed everywhere at night; they didn't. After dark, you didn't know where they might or might not be, and although in the expansive and isolated Central Highlands your chances of encountering them were probably rather slim, no civilian wanted to take that chance (few ARVN units wanted to either, for that matter). What those who considered venturing—or staying—out after dark also knew was that everyone on "our side" buttoned up into such fortifications as they possessed as soon as night fell, if not earlier. Under the cover of night, anyone you encountered might or might not be hostile, but none would be helpful. If you got into trouble, you were SOL (Shit Outta Luck).

Virtually all of the provincial population that we knew about lived close to QL 20 and thus in the "secure" areas. We could travel to just about any population cluster and return, all within that important "day trip" concept. QL 20 had been repaved and was an excellent asphalt roadway, if not very wide and usually lacking in shoulders. We nevertheless had constant problems with getting around on the ground, but they were of our own making. I discovered this truth the hard way because I had to deal with it constantly. It was my side job.

We civilian members of the team had subsidiary assignments in addition to conducting our counterpart relationships. My primary side job, as the lowest-ranking civilian on the province team, was to supervise—and account for in reports—our small fleet of International Harvester Scouts. Both Jim Chrysler and I drove Scouts. Romy had been assigned one, and one of the team's Vietnamese employees, Mr. Thanh, who supervised the other local staff and was responsible for general support activities, including vehicle maintenance, drove one also. Gasoline for our vehicles was trucked in and dispensed at the compound's work area. Mr. Thanh supervised the gas distribution, so some steady loss of fuel occurred, totally off the books, of course. He spoke of the need to "clean our hands," so I knew this was one of those areas that required me to keep watch but largely let things be, only trying to keep gasoline consumption from becoming too obviously excessive. Siphoning off of the Americans' copious material wealth, in this case quite literally, was an understood fact of life at every level.

On the subject of local driving, more needs to be said about the International Harvester Scout. The Scout was the designated vehicle for all civilian government field personnel in Viet Nam except for police advisors. It was also the bane of my existence for the entirety of my two-year tour. I shall ever regard that abomination as the worst vehicle built in the United States. Such a status would put it in the very pits of engineering, no doubt with others perhaps more deserving of the title, but I stand by my claim. There were three other Scouts on the roster, although lacking some part or the other. They were remnants of a busier time. Those three extra Scouts came in handy because either Jim's or mine was undergoing some sort of maintenance pretty much all the time. The constant need for maintenance was the most persistently annoying thing about the Scout. My little fleet of Scouts always seemed to be in constant need of repair, or simply adjustment, most often of that cursed clutch/transmission. The clutch was a constant headache, requiring frequent work. The transmission was balky and did the clutch no good.

A Spear-Carrier in Viet Nam

The heart of the Scout, its engine, was its best part—simple, not over-stressed and reliable. That could not be said of the Scout's other parts. I shall ignore the Scout's tendency to rust and suffer small electric component failures with painful regularity or that damned constantly-in-need-of-adjustment clutch and focus on the Scout's major failure: its total inability to do what an off-road vehicle is supposed to do: get around off the road with a reasonable chance of getting back on the road when it's desired. Considering that this ability had been the primary requirement for choosing a vehicle for Viet Nam, the Scout was perhaps the worst choice available at the time. Out in a province or district off-road travel was a daily necessity, as the few paved roads connected only major towns or base areas. The only requirement in the dry season was a set of off-road tires and the Scout performed acceptably well, but the rainy season was an entirely different matter. Rain on the red clay soil produced a treacly and tenacious mud, and woe betide the careless.

The Scout did have good ground clearance, but its four-wheel drive just didn't do the job. I wasn't mechanically knowledgeable enough to say why this was—it just was. The most annoying part was that engaging the four-wheel drive required exiting the vehicle and turning a central hub on each of the four axles. Turning those hubs when they were dusty or muddy (which pretty much defined their condition during Viet Nam's two seasons) ranged from difficult to impossible. They were designed to be turned by hand, but I on more than one occasion had to resort to external force. This was annoying, but what was worse was that I knew it wasn't going to help much. Even when engaged, the four wheels never seemed to be working together.

The conventional wisdom to explain the disaster that was the Scout was that it had been an inducement offered by LBJ to Illinois senator Everett Dirksen, in whose state they were made, for his support of the war. I always doubted this story, as Senator Dirksen never needed an incentive to vote for a war, but LBJ was adept at rewarding his supporters, so the story may well have been true, if overemphasized. Whatever the reason, Scouts were the vehicles American CORDS civilians drove, period. Police advisors drove civilian (CJ model) Jeeps, and the military members of the team drove M-151 MUTTs (Multipurpose Utility Tactical Transport), which everyone referred to as "jeeps."

I had been warned of the Scout's central deficiency and had been careful. I still managed to plant my Scout in the mud, at the worst possible time, during Ambassador Colby's visit that was to include a briefing by me about Nam Phuong. After the ceremony of giving away the tractors, I drove down to Nam Phuong refugee camp, updating my information. The creek that divided the camp created a short stretch of road that was soft but passable in the dry season but continually muddy during the rainy season. Vehicle traffic over this stretch churned the mix even more. I crossed successfully on my way in but not on my way back out. I had engaged the damn hubs (with great difficulty) before attempting to cross, but it was hopeless. The more I worked it, the deeper it sank. I finally gave up and hitched a ride back to the CORDS compound on a motor scooter driven by a local. There I borrowed a spare Scout and drove to my house. After a quick shower and change of clothes, I drove to the MACV compound and informed Major Brown of what had happened. He couldn't organize a pickup until the next morning, as it was growing dark. A team went out first thing the next morning and returned my Scout, or at least what was left of it, to the CORDS compound. The engine block, transmission, seats, and windshield were still there, but absolutely everything else that could be removed by common tools had been, presumably by the refugees in the camp. I was surprised to see the seats still there, as they were easy to remove. Apparently the Vietnamese thought them as uncomfortable as I did. All four of the wheels and tires were gone, of course. There was no battery, wires, sparkplugs, lightbulbs, carburetor, no nothing.

I thought my Scout was a lost cause, but I didn't factor in the nature of the U.S. supply bureaucracy. An advisory team was allotted a certain number of Scouts, and that was that; they could not be replaced. Parts, however, could be replaced. So my Scout was rebuilt (slowly) as parts were obtained. The process must have more greatly resembled the vehicle's initial construction—minus the assembly line and big machines—than it did anything usually referred to as "repair." My Scout finally did return to the team's use, I am told, but I was long gone by then.

Getting Around in the Air

If we needed to go any farther than a day's drive, we flew. Every American flew virtually everywhere we could, and you could fly almost anywhere, down to the district level. By the time I left in 1972, I also thought myself fortunate that I had to fly in a Vietnamese Air Force (VNAF) aircraft only once. All Americans feared flying in VNAF aircraft, particularly those who did so as a part of their advisory tasks. This wasn't about flying competence—many VNAF pilots were excellent—but more about something that transcended individual personality or ability. It just seemed to be "in the blood." The Vietnamese were superb "shade tree" mechanics, despite the frequent lack of any shade under which to perform their wizardry. That first sight of a motorized cyclo driver intently rebuilding his engine in the middle of downtown Saigon traffic had been repeated countless times against different backgrounds. These people learned about their machines the hard way and managed to keep vehicles running despite a

Saigon transportation: the motorized cyclo.

wholesale lack of spare parts. If the engines always smoked—oh, well, at least they ran.

But it seemed that the Vietnamese could not learn the concept of "preventive maintenance." This was a critical shortcoming for anyone being schooled in the American way of war, but it not only existed—it was also pervasive. Both the Vietnamese military and civilian structure demonstrated this unfortunate trait—over and over—by a combination of having many vehicles off line at any one time and an alarming number of accidents and crashes among those that were in service. Time and time again the fault was traced directly to lack of proper maintenance. We designed, equipped, and installed a complex, interdependent war machine and handed it over to people we knew could not maintain it. There was much more to this than the fact that the machine we left them ran on oil and then the U.S. government cut off their supply. That's true as far as it goes, but even if we had kept them awash in the stuff the system would have broken down.

The vast majority of us always flew Air America. Every province and every district had its own airstrip. Lam Dong's was a simple asphalt stretch with a turnaround at one end and a parking area off to the side. There were additional barrels and bunkers, as the strip hosted the two Huey gunships that, with their crews and maintenance personnel, had been posted to Bao Loc. They were to provide air support should the province or district headquarters—or Team #38's MACV compound—be attacked. It never happened, and the crews were, in truth, bored. One of the pilots once described to me how while he was up flying around he would look for an elephant, or even a tiger, to stalk and shoot. I was appalled, and told him so. His reply was, "You want me to be ready if something happens, right? You want me to have a good aim, right?" I gave up, and dropped the subject.

One Morning in Nha Trang

My previously mentioned dislike of Nha Trang had much to do with the schedules of the flights to and from the town, but I had other reasons also. One of the memories that contributed greatly to my opinion was a day—just a morning, actually—I spent there. It is stored in my nightmare collection. The odd thing is that I cannot remember why I was there. Was

A Spear-Carrier in Viet Nam

I on my way to Saigon or returning to Bao Loc? I seem to have blanked out the contextual details, but my memory of the day itself remains painfully clear. I had spent an uneventful night in the MACV BOQ transient compound, but I awoke the next morning in Bizarro World. Outside the compound itself there was the usual bustle of activity, but I immediately noticed an uncommonly large collection of Vietnamese gathered around open sections of the compound fence. Inside, in considerable contrast, there was nothing—nothing—happening. No buses or any other vehicles were entering or leaving the compound, as was usually the case. Not even people walking about; all was still. Curious, I searched for someone, anyone, to explain. I found a Vietnamese, who told me—in English—that it was "Change Day." This was my first encounter with the expression, and I had no idea what he meant. I would soon learn in the hardest possible way, step by step.

There was a small station within the compound that handled travel arrangements for those temporarily housed there, with which I had dealt before. I spoke to a TCN who was sitting at his desk doing nothing, about whether the shuttle to Saigon would depart on time. He said he didn't know, but it didn't matter, because the bus shuttle to the airport wasn't running. "Why not?," I inquired. "Change Day," was all he said in reply. That explained everything as far as he was concerned. Some context is needed here. I had stumbled, unknowingly, into one of the many means by which we attempted to deal with the obscene amount of money we were pouring into an economy utterly incapable of dealing with the invasion. Viet Nam was neither the first nor the last such economy to which we brought these issues, but it has to be among the most totally affected. The relationship between the dollar and the piaster was officially established and universally ignored. This was more than a "black market." Any American could find a Vietnamese willing to accept American money for anything. Thousands of American soldiers, on leave or between assignments, quickly found out that while they may have been poor in American terms, they were rich over here. This overwhelmed the local economy, with wholly unfortunate results.

Fully aware of the problem, the embassy had forbidden the possession or use of U.S. currency by Americans, whether military or civilian, in Viet Nam. Upon arrival in country, you were required to exchange your dollars for scrip: pieces of paper that bore an uncanny resemblance to Monopoly money and were almost as small. This scrip was, at least theoretically, much less popular than real dollars because it could not be exchanged for any real currency. That may very well have been true, but regardless of its external convertibility scrip simply became the means of exchange between corrupt Americans and corruptible Vietnamese, an internal currency with validity throughout South Viet Nam, if no farther. The black market functioned with scrip just as well as it had with real dollars, or so it seemed.

One means of combatting this was to periodically change the scrip. Americans—and only Americans—could exchange old scrip for new, in exactly the same amounts, of course. This took place on "Change Day," and that date was easily the best-kept secret of the entire war, if we are talking about keeping it secret from the Americans. Change Day was probably just as much a surprise to the Vietnamese, but they always reacted quickly because they had to. By day's end, their scrip would be worth nothing. After "Change Day," there was literally no market for yesterday's scrip. This meant that for the Americans all, repeat all, exchanges had to take place on Change Day. The reasons for this were obvious, understood by all, and just as universally misallocated. It was all about catching those crooked, thieving Vietnamese off-guard, we said. I don't recall anyone ever mentioning that every piece of scrip a Vietnamese possessed had to have originated with an American.

Thwarting those thieving locals required sealing the American compounds off from all physical contact during "Change Day." No cars or buses arrived or left, because none were allowed to. I can only imagine now what the scene outside an American military base must have been like; back then I was caught up in a much smaller world, locked inside a civilian base in Nha Trang. This accounted for the people—all Vietnamese, of course—I had seen gathered at open places in the fence, i.e., where small things could be exchanged through the chain links. Each person, both male and female, clutched handfuls of scrip and was thrusting them forward. These people were too late, as any stretch of fence open enough for approaching was exposed to all eyes, including American ones inside whose job it was to see and identify those Americans who might approach the fence. No one inside even went near the fence. In fact, no one inside went anywhere. It was just too suspicious an action on Change Day. Everyone kept to his room or to his office if he was within that compound, which explained the complete lack of activity I had found so baffling.

The object of locking down American sites was to ensure that no one could access any off-site sources of scrip, namely those anxious Vietnamese who possessed some. Enterprising Americans would have bought it for pennies on the dollar and exchanged it for a nice profit. The problem for me—and, I suspect, for anyone else so unfortunate as to be travelling on Change Day—was that you could change your scrip only at the location from which you had obtained it in the first place. At least that was what I was told, although I thereafter questioned how such an inconvenient system could be applied to everyone. This meant that there was no need to go anywhere on Change Day; you just exchanged your scrip at the compound's "bank." CORDS compounds, whether office or residential, had such locations. Even Bao Loc had one, but that didn't help me in Nha Trang, at this transient location. I found myself sealed into a location that was not the source of my scrip. I was a man outside the assigned bureaucratic structure, in one of those small cracks into which I managed to plummet on more than one occasion.

The Americans at this compound weren't going to do anything and absent their approval neither were the Vietnamese lounging around. Neither was the TCN I spoke to at his office, where travel arrangements were confirmed. Was I stuck there another day? Yes. Can you schedule me on tomorrow's flight? No, we have no information about that. Are you really sure that the Air America shuttles are not running? No. How about the bus shuttle to the CORDS office compound? Not running; nothing is. Where can I get something to eat? At the canteen over there, but they may not accept your old scrip anymore. I walked to the canteen, where they were uncertain about accepting my scrip (these were Vietnamese, doubly isolated by circumstances). After some discussion, my money was accepted and I breakfasted. It was a good thing I did, because by noon my money was no good. After I discovered my scrip was no longer good at the small compound PX, all I wanted to do was get out of there. I resolved to find out if any flights were actually happening. At that point, the flight could have been to just about anywhere as far as I was concerned.

My problem was that I was operating on a complete lack of information. With my Vietnamese, I could get to the airport but would any planes be flying? And if not, what would I do next? The safest thing would have been to just sit in place until tomorrow. No one could suspect me of anything if I just sat around in my room (and didn't approach the fence), and going without dinner would not hurt me very much. But by that time I was furious at what I had already identified as a specific source of personal irritation: government bureaucracy. By this I mean the pig-headed insistence on placing each and every person within a specific box that fit seamlessly into the structural flow chart. The possibility that there could be exceptions to the bureaucratically determined alternatives was simply denied; you were squeezed and molded until you fit into a box. I was beginning to comprehend that this was going to be a very long war. So I left. I just packed up my small bag and walked out the compound gate. No one tried to stop me, although I'm sure they would have if I had tried to return. Once outside the gate, I was besieged by Vietnamese clawing at me, trying to get my attention. Some unexpected directives from this American in their own language gave me enough room to get away and into a small pedal cyclo. "The airport," I told him. It wasn't a quick ride, but at least I was out of Bizarro World. The fact that I may have been just leaving one to go to another occurred to me, but I felt it was worth it. When we arrived at a pedestrian gate, my driver tried to get me to pay in new scrip, of course. Actually, he wanted to exchange his old for my new, dollar for dollar. I declined, explaining that I didn't have any new scrip, but of course he didn't believe me. He finally, after much weeping and gnashing of teeth, agreed to accept my piasters. So far, so good, but what would I find at the airstrip? To my enormous relief (and considerable surprise), flights were still taking off, but everything was late, not surprisingly. Best of all, the daily southern shuttle flight had not yet left. I got on and was never before or again so happy to be flying in a C-47 over the southern highlands. And yes, I was able to exchange my scrip at my team HQ.

Visitors

While out in my Scout one morning, I received a call from the TOC telling me to report to the airstrip, as an inbound flight wanted to see me. I had absolutely no idea what this was, but I complied and drove up to the airstrip. Upon arrival, the radio office (I can't call it "air traffic control") told me the flight's arrival was imminent. Just a few minutes later a U.S. military Huey helicopter appeared from out of the west and set down on that portion of the asphalt side strips laid out for them. I walked over to greet it, and once the rotor had settled down a little out stepped my father. I hadn't seen him since my arrival in Bao Loc, although I knew he was then serving as DPSA in Phuoc Long Province. Although Phuoc Long bordered Cambodia and was in III Corps, it was actually west of Lam Dong, hence the direction of the helicopter's arrival.

While such a father-son reunion must have been rare in Viet Nam (particularly for civilians), it was by no means unheard of, but what happened next put me in a very rare category: my mother stepped out of the helicopter. She was in country to visit my father, who being the DPSA, was able to utilize one of the choppers assigned to the advisory team to just swing out of both province and region to see me. It was a brief visit, as it was about as unauthorized as a flight could be. We hugged, spoke briefly, and then they were off. As their helicopter took off it struck me how weird it was that my parents, who could not come to either my college graduation or my wedding, could drop in to see me in the middle of Viet Nam. What a difference half a world makes.

In early September I heard from Barbara that she would interview for a job in Saigon with a company called Control Data. She would be flying there later in the month and wanted to join me in Lam Dong province after her interview. I was pleased, of course, and got my father to arrange her flights to Bao Loc. Things were still in full swing at Nam Phuong, and I did not feel I could get away for the time the travel schedule required. Barbara didn't mind; this was the kind of adventure she had hoped for when she had decided she wanted to work abroad. And so it came to be that in late September Barbara stepped off the southern shuttle at Bao Loc airstrip, where I was waiting for her. She moved into my house, and I began to show her around. She remained until early October and got a good glimpse of how things actually worked. I introduced her to Mr. Khiem as a matter of courtesy. I drove her around, and she heartily agreed with my conclusion that this was a beautiful area. I showed her the town, my refugee site, and even got in a drive down the B'Sar Pass, beautiful, scenic, and twisty, past small waterfalls, plus strange plants and trees galore. She charmed everyone, and before she left Colonel Thoms gave her a certificate declaring her to be an honorary lifetime member of Advisory Team #38, for her work as "morale booster."

Barbara got the job and moved to Saigon. She was also able to fly up for the Christmas/New Year's holidays and had a great time, with parties at my house, the MILPHAP house, and the MACV compound. The party at the MACV compound was one to remember. Colonel Thompson and his senior staff manned the perimeter that night (in full battle array), so the younger officers could party—which they did. The only problem on this second visit was that Barbara had brought her Siamese cat, Xin Loi

(*Excuse Me* in Vietnamese), with her, and it had been held in Nha Trang for quarantine. It did not arrive by the time she had to return, early in the New Year.

Road Warrior

Now that Barbara was living in Saigon I was looking more intently for a solution to my transportation problem, and the final straw came about two weeks after her departure. On that day, the TOC summoned me to the airstrip, for reasons again unspecified. When I arrived, I found waiting for me Barbara's Siamese cat, which had been held in quarantine for the entire holiday period and then some. He became my housemate but was appropriately standoffish. I expected to start seeing some cockroach corpses in my bathroom now that Xin Loi was making his nocturnal rounds. I did, but only a few, and I knew that a great many more live specimens were lurking not far away. I began to wonder if Xin Loi had, in true Vietnamese fashion, found a method of ignoring the enemy during the night. He was no difficulty to take care of and I didn't mind having him around, but he was Barbara's cat and she wanted him back. So, just how was I going to get this damn cat back to Saigon? If I flew the shuttle to Nha Trang, the beast would likely be separated from me and stranded again in that unpleasant town. Besides, I had grown thoroughly sick of the two-shuttles-with-an-overnight-between-them trip to Saigon. There had to be a better way.

My search for an alternative to the Region II shuttle had already led me to try a regularly scheduled Australian military plane nicknamed the "Wallaby." The plane was a DeHavilland Caribou, a high-winged STOL craft well suited to visiting the small airstrips that dotted the countryside. Its departure from Bao Loc was actually the last leg of a regularly scheduled round-trip flight from Saigon. The Wallaby apparently existed to service the various Australian locations around the country. I had no idea why it stopped in Bao Loc, as we had no Australians, but it did. I flew it only once and had the pleasurable experience of viewing the countryside from the rear, as the loadmaster left the tailgate down (he said he always did, he enjoyed the view). Unfortunately, it flew only once a week, on Fridays, and in only one direction, south. That meant I would have to use the Nha Trang shuttle to return. The Wallaby didn't provide what I needed.

A Spear-Carrier in Viet Nam

The cat was the final straw. I began to look seriously into an option that had been obvious from the first but that no one had ever tried: drive to Saigon and back. The fact that I even considered taking such a chance on the Scout is testimony to how much I hated the shuttle, or more accurately the required overnight in Nha Trang. Theoretically, what I proposed to do was quite simple. The distance between Bao Loc and Saigon was just under 100 miles. I would have to drive a considerably more circuitous route, cross a couple of rivers and in general follow a line on a map that was remarkably devoid of details, a considerably longer trip. At least I wasn't going to get lost. QL20 was a two-lane blacktop road, and relatively busy through Lam Dong. A wide variety of commercial trucks, several buses, and even private automobiles passed through Bao Loc every day, bound either north or south. If the Vietnamese could drive this route regularly and without incident, why couldn't I? The trip just didn't strike me as that dangerous. QL 20 was a heavily traveled road dawn to dusk. The length of the trip was unknown, as no local American had ever traveled it before, but it should require less than a day and that day, even with considerable allowance built in for delays en route.

At first, Jim Chrysler was incredulous that I even wanted to do such a thing. No American on the MACV team had ever even considered it nor known anyone else who had. Americans going any distance always flew; it was what we did. Still, he checked with the colonel, who did not object. They did not exactly encourage me, but they did not forbid me to take the Scout out of province as they could have. They did remind me that I was venturing into the unknown, as no American civilian had ever attempted what I proposed to do. I planned on a long weekend trip, driving down Friday and returning on Sunday. On the appointed day, I loaded my Scout (which I had just sent through "maintenance") for the journey, and made sure I had a full tank of gas. I did take along my M-2 carbine, but I stowed it down in the very back of the Scout and put the clip in the glove compartment. I just didn't see myself shooting it out with anyone.

I decided to make the journey as pleasant as possible and stocked a portable cooler with some ice and water. I then opened and recorked a bottle of white wine and placed it down into the cooler. I kept an unopened bottle for the trip back, along with a corkscrew. I took a plastic cup for the actual drinking of it. I put Xin Loi into his cage, then put it in the backseat, locked my house door, and departed. This was one of the few times I reported in to the TOC, as I would be exiting the province. The drive down B'Sar Pass was always fun. I loved to fancy myself as Stirling Moss throwing my Scout around the corners. Neither the vehicle nor the driver were anywhere near to that standard, but hey, I could pretend. I exited B'Sar Pass and was quickly out of Lam Dong and the highlands, pretty much simultaneously. The next province south was Long Khanh, through which I had to drive, and then Bien Hoa Province before reaching the Gia Dinh/Saigon area. I soon concluded that Xin Loi, who had begun yelling as only Siamese cats can yell shortly after we left and had not stopped, was not going to. He did not, the entire trip. Once out of the highlands, I figured the road was pretty much straight and not too twisty from here on as I gradually descended from a plain down to the delta, so it was time to break out the wine.

QL 20 was, by Vietnamese standards, going to be a major, properly built road at some point in the future, thanks to the U.S. Army engineers. That meant a well-graded road built with good quality asphalt, but still only two lanes, plus graded shoulders. Most of the road was already that, but not all of it. As I passed those areas still under construction, I joined the other traffic shunted to a parallel service road. These were only roughly graded and were surfaced with oiled stone to keep the dust down. The oil did so, to some extent, but also caused much of the black gravel torn up by my tires to stick to various parts of the Scout. Traffic invariably backed up along these stretches, so I drove each in close company with other vehicles, mostly civilian trucks. Once past a stretch being worked on, we were directed back onto the main road and proceeded until we came to the next unfinished segment, where we repeated the experience. Each of the bridges over the rivers that QL 20 crossed while in Long Khanh and Bien Hoa provinces had been destroyed, and their replacements were not yet completed. That meant a diversion down the oiled dirt service road to a pontoon bridge across the water and onto another service road for some distance afterward before rejoining the road itself. As I drove over the pontoon bridge in the shadow of the new bridge but within sight of the old, destroyed French bridge still lying across the river, I wondered about just how long this new bridge was going to last.

While driving down QL 20 in Long Khanh, I saw ahead of me an American soldier standing on the side of the road, M-16 in hand, actually hitching a ride. This was a reassuring sign about the local security situation, and I pulled over. He was an enlisted man from a U.S. engineer battalion stationed just down the road, hot and sweat-soaked, and he wanted to get back to his hooch. I rolled down the passenger window. "Where're you going?" I asked. He just stood there, his eyes as wide as saucers, trying to take in what he was seeing. "Ju … just down the road," he managed to say. "Get in, I'll take you there," I replied. He climbed in, put his M-16 on the floor in front of him and looked around at the civilian giving him a ride, the open cooler with wine bottles, and the cat howling in the backseat. "Want some wine? Here, have some," I said as I handed him a cup. I drove off, with him sitting there, his eyes still uncomprehending. The trip didn't take long. He spoke up as we neared a gate and some barbed wire, and I dropped him off. He didn't take the unfinished cup of wine and he didn't even gulp down the last of it; he just handed it over to me with that blank stare.

Along the way, the presence of U.S. military vehicles increased steadily. Initially they had been largely from engineer units camped nearby, but as I got into southern Long Khanh it became more general, hauling material rather than machines. The road had, in fact, become quite busy, which it remained until I got onto the Saigon-Bien Hoa Highway, which produced levels of traffic worthy of the busiest road in the U.S. of almost entirely trucks. I reached Saigon with no issues, then found—with greater difficulty—the location of Barbara's apartment. This was an eye-opening experience. The trip had only taken a few hours. A few hours to go some 100 miles doesn't sound like much, but in the environment of Viet Nam at the time it was amazing. I had found a quick way to make the trip, and had a vehicle to drive around while in Saigon. No schedule to meet, no nothing. I could leave when I wanted to. I no longer had to take that damned shuttle with the overnight in Nha Trang, and I never did again, save on my formal departure from province, when I obviously couldn't drive. While I was sorely tempted to utilize this new discovery to spend my weekends in Saigon, my sense of duty intervened. I drove down every two or three weeks, depending on my schedule. Once I was sure of the route and of the time required—with some allowance for delays—I could leave Friday afternoon and return Sunday afternoon.

The Final Months

I had all this free time because when I first discovered I could drive to Saigon it was rather late in my time in Lam Dong, after things fell into a stasis. Still, being a member of a small team I felt responsibility for doing my share, regardless of anything else. Administering our "fleet" of Scouts had been the main one and it continued, but I also volunteered to perform other advisory tasks. Finding other tasks was not a problem, but there was one hitch. The projects that required effort to initiate, reform, or sustain were development ones, and community development officers were the people assigned to them. Team #38 had no such officer, and an array of young military officers had arrived, attempted to cope with tasks for which they had no training, and then departed, leaving things largely the same. I was available and as far as training goes I was better equipped at VTC to do development work than refugee work. Still, I was a relief/rehabilitation officer, and to that slot I was firmly attached. It was all about "slots," and personal considerations never entered the picture. I could perform the work in province with the Vietnamese, but I could not formally request items, fill out reports, or do anything that travelled in American circles, as I was not properly titled and occupied the wrong slot in the command structure. I thus began to ask the question of just exactly what was I doing—as in "accomplishing"—in Lam Dong? That question would hang over my remaining time in province.

I wasn't all that unhappy about not being able to fill out reports, of course. One of them would have been the dreaded Hamlet Evaluation System, or HES. Everyone I spoke with who had some part in preparing that report remarked on how little it reflected the reality of the situation. It was all about putting an infinite humanity into a limited number of slots according to strict criteria, i.e., bureaucracy run rampant. This meant it also became part of the unspoken—and almost unconscious—general will to believe that we were "winning" the war. DPSA Jim Chrysler had been handling the development tasks, at least as far as reporting to Saigon was concerned. I spoke to him of my desire to fill my steadily increasing free time, and he agreed gladly but warned me that I would be helping to "just piss away money." By this he meant that our development projects weren't accomplishing much, but they were cheap compared to the money we were throwing away on other things.

He had already told me of one example, the largest project in the province, during my initial orientation tour with him. This was a tea-processing factory of some size, "the largest tea factory in Southeast Asia," Jim had been told. It was surrounded by stout fencing, and as we drove around I could vaguely see the outlines of machinery inside. The gate was locked, because nothing was happening inside this impressive, still-new-looking structure. The factory had been built before his arrival, he said, so he knew things only by hearsay. This had been one of the classic USAID projects. A good deal of money had been spent, but the factory had operated for about only one week before shutting down and had never reopened. He didn't know why and said nobody else professed to know either. So there it sat, a white elephant if there ever was one.

In the following months, I would drive by on occasion to check its status. I thought it remarkable that such a project on which a substantial amount of money had been invested just sat there, with no one doing anything about it. I thought it equally remarkable that it had not been plundered, as was the fate of virtually everything once the Americans lost interest. I never learned exactly why the factory was such a bust. In fact, I never heard anything further about it at all. Whatever the reason(s) for its specific demise, that beautiful but useless tea factory was a classic example of USAID/CORDS's lack of any means to sustain projects. The fact that only a short time after its construction no American in province

Pissing away money: The silent, unused Bao Loc tea factory, 1971.

knew anything about its history demonstrated our complete lack of institutional memory. Advisors came and advisors went, to province after province and district after district, with no attempt to collect or transmit information from those who had learned the hard way, assuring that their successors would have to repeat the experience.

Duroc Pigs and American Know-How

Jim also related to me the saga of the Duroc pigs. Like virtually every American idea-turned-policy, it began with good intentions and addressed a real problem. And like virtually every one of them it foundered along the way, largely by drawing up a plan based on American reality, not that of Viet Nam. The need to improve the quality of the four-legged swine of Viet Nam was obvious to all, whether you worked with Vietnamese or Montagnards. The Vietnamese pot-bellied pig would later become a trendy American pet, but in Viet Nam they were pests—filthy, free-roaming carriers of hookworm. The American answer was a program to demonstrate to a Vietnamese farmer how to raise a better (American) pig, breed them, and then sell them for a profit. We selected the Duroc breed and sent several to Viet Nam (Jim didn't know how many or where else they had been sent), accompanied by detailed instructions on how to raise the pig. A pig such as a Duroc could not be allowed to roam freely but had to be confined, largely because it also had to be fed a special diet. Jim told me of how a few local Vietnamese farmers had been selected as recipients of the pigs and given the instructions and the necessary food. This was a year-long project that was monitored by both GVN and American officials. The results should have been obvious from the start, but that would have meant the project would never have been implemented in the first place. The pigs did grow to a size unseen in Viet Nam and were both admired and prized. Unfortunately, the cost of their feed greatly exceeded the price their meat would bring on the local Vietnamese market. Success had been assumed, with no provision to continue subsidizing the farmers after the initial year, so the project was short-lived. The original pigs were slaughtered, their meat sold at a loss, and that was that.

I remember one other development project quite well, despite the fact that I had nothing to do with it, my exposure to it lasted one day, and I only watched. It was not a CORDS project at all but purely a military "civic action" one. The U.S. military unit involved was an engineer battalion stationed just south of Lam Dong, one of several rebuilding QL 20. The project's location was in Lam Dong's southernmost section, a village called Madaguoi. Madaguoi was a Montagnard village, all of which were neglected, but its distance from Bao Loc made it even more neglected than most. Some engineer officer had doubtless driven past the village (it was visible from QL 20) and resolved to use American technology to help "those poor people."

The project was to be a dam along the local creek in order to provide water for irrigation. It was to be a simple earthen structure. It slanted inward on both sides, was fortified with rocks amid the earth and built within a cage of bamboo stalks tied to one another to form a grid that would serve to guide the deposited earth and rock into the proper shape and resist erosion. The dam was to be built by local people using local materials. The work required a diversion channel for the creek's water while the dam was being constructed, and that was where the U.S. engineers came in. They were going to dig that diversion channel as the project got underway.

On the appointed day I drove down B'Sar Pass to observe their work. Upon my arrival, the expanse of bone-dry field with withered brown plants at intervals along the rows testified to the need for water. The engineers were already there, in the form of a multi-wheel excavator, the type with a telescoping arm, and a few other vehicles. A number of Montagnard men in loincloths and each with a rough hoe sat nearby. They were to finish the work after the excavator had dug the rough channel then begin the dam. But there was a problem. The excavator had made it up QL 20 from Long Khanh, but that was all it was going to do. It had "broken down" was all the explanation I could get. A wrecker had been called to tow it, and in the meanwhile the engineers were just standing around. This did not seem to faze the officer in charge, who confidently proclaimed, "No problem. We'll just use C-4 to blast a channel." We all obediently withdrew some distance while a soldier planted some C-4 in the ground. A loud explosion followed by clouds of red dust resulted. When the dust cleared, we all saw that the C-4 had made virtually no impression on the solidly packed red clay. Burying it a few inches produced only a small, and very shallow, crater. Lacking any drills, C-4 was clearly not the answer. By noon, American know-how had taken it in the ear, and badly. As the Americans stood around waiting to get out of there, that group of Montagnard men with hoes who were supposed to perform the finishing touches began to do the heavy work themselves. By late afternoon when I left, primitive people wielding equally primitive technology had largely accomplished what modern technology had so utterly failed to do, and the diversion channel was taking shape.

I returned later to observe the dam being built, and discovered that reality had failed to measure up to promise yet again. The diversion channel could not be made watertight at the point of intersection, and water constantly leaked out, soaking the base of the dam as it was being built. Everybody knew this was going to be a problem, but no one deviated from the program. Some water backed up at the dam and irrigating the nearby fields became easier, but by the time I departed for Saigon the dam had clearly been added to that enormous list of "what might have been" in Viet Nam.

Despite my not being an official development advisor, I was allowed to attend a Region II conference of such officers in, as I remember, Pleiku. I got to meet some of the people whose names I had heard of but had never encountered. Also attending the conference was George Jacobsen, Colby's deputy, famous for killing with his pistol the last VC who had penetrated the U.S. embassy compound in the early hours of Tet of '68.

I was well aware of my semi-status, so I kept quiet. Several USAID development types from Saigon also attended, and most of the conference was spent with them pitching their plans for the "next phase" of the counterinsurgency program, building on the success we had experienced, etc., etc. During this time I noticed that virtually none of the provincial level advisors—those who actually knew what was going on—had anything to contribute. By late afternoon I had just about had all of this bullshit I could take and seized on an opening provided by another province advisor who had the temerity to question an assumption of the presentation we had just heard. I employed a little piece of nonsense the advisory team had received by memo to illustrate my point.

My job of overseeing our small fleet of Scouts had delivered a lesson on how assumptions about "winning" can transmit nonsense down the bureaucratic channels. It was a memo from Saigon, some damn agency concerned with supplying our Scouts. Its message was that, in recognition of the improved security situation nationwide and the accompanying improvement in the road system, no more off-road tires would be supplied to province teams, only road tires. I don't know who came up with such a dumb idea, but it had clearly been no one with field experience in Viet Nam. In our Scouts, road tires off a road would have been useless. The whole thing stank of some bureaucrat far away from the action making decisions on the basis of our questionable reports about pacification's progress. This was a silly little thing, one of a thousand I probably encountered, but it has always stuck in my memory as testimony to the absurdity of American assumptions about what we were doing here.

Using the road tires memo as my opening, I basically denounced the entire meeting as a similar exercise in fantasy. I then admitted that I really shouldn't be saying these things, as I was officially unqualified to have an opinion. Out of the corner of my eye I saw George Jacobsen choking on his cigar with laughter. He was another friend of my father's, and I had made another impression, evidently a good one. It seems I did with my fellow provincial officers also, as later that evening at the officer's club, the other provincial advisors refused to let me pay for a drink and foisted several on me. Virtually every one of them knew a great deal more about the reality of Viet Nam than I did, but only I had had the temerity to say it out loud. I was never sure whether that was good or bad.

As my official workload in Lam Dong dwindled, I kept WVD Saigon well informed of the deteriorating situation, hoping that they could somehow break the bureaucratic logjam. They, realizing, I thought, that a personnel asset was underemployed, responded in late May 1971 by ordering my departure from Advisory Team 38 and reassignment to Saigon. I confess to mixed feelings upon hearing the news. I most definitely looked forward to living with Barbara, but the Nam Phuong project had stalled, leaving me with a bad aftertaste to what had been an excellent beginning. But there were no further prospects for me in Lam Dong. I had mixed feelings about a Saigon assignment, for sure. As was standard procedure for every region, province, and district level civilian CORDS officer, I had come to despise "those bureaucrats" in Saigon, who, it seemed, were slow to respond to requests for actual help, being only interested in reports. I had fallen into this, which in a world characterized by inadequate communication methods between levels meant seeing only your side of the picture. I was quite quickly to be introduced to the other side and worked within it for the remainder of my tour.

My leave-taking was decidedly low key, just brief good-byes to each member of the team, beginning with Colonel Thompson and Mr. Khiem, of course. Just turn over the keys to the house and the Scout, load my footlocker once again, and then get a ride to the Bao Loc airstrip. The process of people arriving and departing the team was quite routine, and it wasn't any big thing even for one of the few civilians. I was lost in thought as I left and didn't pay much attention to the flight back or even the overnight stay in Nha Trang. As things turned out, I never again saw any member of Advisory Team #38 except for Fred Gymball, on a visit to Saigon, as I will relate. I was going only a few miles away, but I was entering another world.

FIVE

Saigon
July 1971–July 1972

WVD

My transfer to Saigon meant that I would be working at the War Victims Directorate (WVD) in USAID II, the headquarters for CORDS programs. The building itself was older but had been retrofitted with air conditioning. It had a small snack bar on the ground floor just outside the building and adjacent to the motor pool. This was actually the rear of the building, but as I never entered any other way it became the front for me. The motor pool sat just behind the entrance gate, which was kept closed, and every vehicle entering was subject to the sweeps for explosives that had become part of the everyday scene. Several cars, all Fords and all painted black, were kept in the lot. Vietnamese chauffeurs, all women, drove the higher ranks to and from work every day, plus any visits to counterpart offices, of course. The WVD's largest component was the Refugee Division. There was also a Rehabilitation Division, with a small staff that worked more or less independently. The Refugee Division had a sizable staff in Saigon and representatives at each regional headquarters in addition to its provincial personnel scattered about the country.

The head of the War Victims Directorate at that time was Jackson Swart, a tall, handsome man with a head of hair that was almost leonine. I never learned anything about his background or how he got the job. He proudly displayed a photo of him and JFK together on the wall behind his desk, which was suggestive. He certainly had not earned the position on the basis of his administrative abilities. While Jackson Swart certainly projected a positive aura, he quickly dissipated it when he opened his mouth. Swart had a position of great responsibility in the face of enormous suf-

128

fering but had no idea of what he was doing, let alone how to do it. His sole leadership effort consisted of periodically calling a staff member into his office for a heartfelt one-on-one talk, and I was the victim of one such. He spent several minutes orating more than speaking to me. He spoke passionately about "these desperate people!" but had absolutely nothing specific to propose. He pleaded—literally pleaded—for my help, gesticulating wildly, but that was it. I left his office a great deal more disturbed than when I had entered it. I once met another staff member leaving Mr. Swart's office just after he had been subjected to this treatment. As he walked past, he shook his head and said to me, "We're on a rudderless ship!" I knew exactly what he meant.

Jackson Swart's deputy, Norman Hearns, was the exact opposite. If Jackson Swart was all glossy appearance and pressed corners, Norman Hearns was dull and round. Everything about him was round, from his head to every curve on his body, and he always spoke softly and with restraint. Jackson Swart was a political appointee, but Norman Hearns was a professional bureaucrat. He never raised his voice or offered more than a conventional gesture or two while talking. While I was already developing a dislike for the species, with Jackson Swart as our director, a bureaucrat like Norman Hearns was exactly what we needed. Saigon was rife with bureaucratic power plays, as the civilian drawdown was now on in earnest, with people leaving daily. The resulting small vacuums of power were contested as survivors of the latest reduction in force (RIF) sought out areas to expand their authority. I did not appreciate this initially, but later I would be quite grateful for Norm Hearns's ability to maneuver within the bureaucracy.

Roy Fontall, the chief of the Refugee Division, was a short, dark-haired man with glasses and an intense, sincere manner. He had been a priest but had left the order and married a Vietnamese woman with whom he lived in Saigon. I had met Roy when I first arrived, had briefed him at Nam Phuong, and would now be working for him directly. I knew immediately that Roy truly cared, and I never saw anything to change my mind during the just over a year that I worked for him. I greatly respected him and his commitment. Roy took me on a courtesy visit to our counterpart GVN organization, the Ministry of Social Welfare (MSW), and introduced me to the principal players. My visit with the ministry's director (whose name I forgot almost immediately) left me with only one memory, an image of him sitting at his desk. He was thin, with skin drawn tautly over his face, nattily dressed, and presided over a desk with only two piles of files neatly stacked on it, neither very high. The skin of his hands was drawn equally taut, but what I remember most was the little finger of his right hand, or more precisely the fingernail. It was at least two inches long, with a pronounced downward curve. I inwardly marveled at how careful—and how cared for—he must have been, to grow such a nail. I immediately recognized the symbolism: here was a French bureaucrat in every way except for that little oriental statement the long fingernail made: "This man does not have to do any physical labor."

The MSW was organized into two divisions, but its divisions were Operations and Logistics. My introductory tour included brief visits with the head of each division. Both were named Ba. Major Ba headed Operations and Lt. Col. Ba headed Logistics. These were their first names of course, and they were not related. I got to know Major Ba rather well. He was active, making frequent inspection trips into the field (a rarity for any high-ranking GVN civilian agency), friendly, and cooperative with Americans. Above all, he was honest, at least as far as anyone could tell. Roy respected him immensely, and some time later, as I transitioned to Major Ba's primary American counterpart, so did I.

Lt. Col. Ba, who headed MSW Logistics, was the exact opposite in every way. He wanted nothing to do with Americans and made that quite clear during my first—and only—visit to his office. This courtesy visit on our part was marked by remarkably little courtesy on his. Roy and I were ushered into his office only after a wait, despite the appointment having been made in advance. Lt. Col. Ba had nothing to say after the greetings, and he always addressed his interpreter, not us, as translation protocol is supposed to require. On the way over Roy had told me that Lt. Col. Ba was considered by everyone to be a crook and pretty much the last person you wanted in charge of collecting and distributing a large number of commodities that were marketable elsewhere. Logistics was where the bottlenecks occurred in relief supplies, but Americans were forbidden to enter "his" warehouses. But he was never shy in asking—through subordinates, as he never contacted his American counterparts directly—for supplies that lay in our warehouses. I saw Lt. Col. Ba only one more time, under circumstances that I will discuss later.

I would be filling the WVD slot formerly occupied by George Korn, a large, squarely built man in his late twenties I met only briefly as I arrived and he departed. Barbara and I were immediately assigned to occupy the apartment George and his wife were leaving. The apartment building was located on Ngo thoi Nhiem Street, just off Cong Ly Street, the major road from downtown to Tan Sun Nhut Airport. This was a convenient connection, but traffic on Cong Ly Street could be horrendous. We Americans had failed to implant many concepts but succeeded in establishing the "rush hour" beyond our wildest expectations. The apartment building was large and built in the American style and had to be quite recent, as the exterior walls had openings for air conditioners and the whole building sat on stilts, making the first floor a covered parking area. This was most welcome during the rainy season. The apartment came complete with a maid, as we inherited George's, who remained to work for us.

George and his gorgeous wife departed, shortly after I arrived in Saigon, and flew to Europe. They had purchased two Triumph motorcycles through PACEX (more about this acronym later) and were going to pick them up in England and tour that country and the continent. They departed, and I never heard anything of them again. I hope all went well for them both. I inherited a great deal more from George than his slot and his apartment. He also solved any questions about transportation when he simply turned over the keys to his jeep, which became mine. Actually, it belonged to our counterpart organization, the MSW, but had been assigned by someone long forgotten to George, who simply passed it on to me. One of the best things was that I only had to go to the MSW's Logistic Compound to have it refilled with gas, at no charge. The jeep was an obvious relic. George told me that it was, in fact, one of the infamous "Green Jeeps," an early example of the interaction of American naivety and Asian cupidity. The story of these was known by pretty much everyone back then, but I never saw anything actually written into the record about them and the whole thing may have well disappeared down the memory hole of historical trivia, so here goes.

It seems that early in the American advisory presence it was realized that one of the multitude of the GVN's shortcomings was a lack of vehicles to transport its officials out into the countryside, which is where we wanted them to go, or at least between home and work, which is more what they had in mind, I am sure. Casting about for a supply of vehicles rugged enough to drive the roads of Viet Nam as they were then meant Jeeps, and someone found a sizeable stock in storage in South Korea. These were Korean War surplus, which probably meant WWII surplus also. A deal was struck whereby the U.S. government purchased a couple hundred of these vehicles (all of which, of course, had once been U.S. government material themselves and simply given to the Koreans). They were to be inspected, serviced as necessary to make them drivable, and then painted. All of them were, in fact, painted, a bilious shade of green. Whatever else was done was done solely to disguise the problems each vehicle had, such as putting sawdust in the gearbox to muffle the sounds of well-worn gears not engaging correctly. The whole affair was a disaster, as the jeeps were virtually unusable. But the money was paid, of course, and all else eventually forgotten. Yet my jeep was not only in good shape, it was also rock reliable. The reason for this was the most important of my many inheritances from George, a Vietnamese man named Nguyen van Trong.

Nguyen van Trong was between forty and fifty years old (by my estimate) when I met him, and tall for a Vietnamese. He told me, in pieces, of his early years; how he had joined the Viet Minh in the struggle against the French but had then turned against "the Communists," as he phrased it. I never found out just why; he was very tight about his past. He worked for the MSW and lived with his wife and two children in one of the semi-slums that had grown up around old Saigon. George had told me of him and then introduced us. Trong had been enormously useful to George, and George told me he was sure I would feel the same. That turned out to be true. I saw Trong only on occasion, and most of those were to ask some favor or another. Yet I had only to contact him and he would see that it was done, somehow.

A good example of Trong's usefulness was my jeep. George had credited him with arranging all the necessary maintenance, as everyone wanted to avoid any "maintenance" done by the MSW. I continued to do this with perfect satisfaction. Then, with the Saigon rainy season approaching, Barbara quite sensibly pointed out that the jeep's standard top-and-rear canvas covering would not provide much protection in a driving monsoon. She asked me to have the sides covered as well, with usable doors. As I had never seen a vehicle so equipped in Saigon, let alone know someone who could do it, I consulted Trong. This was a tough one, even for him. It took him several days to locate someone—somewhere in Saigon/Cholon—who could do the work. I gave him the jeep and decided to use the shuttle bus which went to USAID II and stopped at our apartment complex in the interim. About a week later, Trong returned the jeep, complete with brand-new canvas top, rear, and sides (in a nicer shade of green), with doors. The doorframes were metal rods, with canvas sewn over them.

The soft plastic side windows could be unzipped on the sides and top, helping to compensate for the fact that enclosing a jeep in Saigon only made it much hotter inside. When the rains came, the new top quickly proved its worth. It had been expensive (by the standard of local expenditures), but I had paid the bill without hesitation, to Trong, of course. I did pay in piasters, by the way. Trong had probably profited from his work, as I fully expected him to do, so I did not inquire about any details of the expense.

The jeep's new canvas illustrates the type of help Trong was only too eager to provide. Trong and I had what can best be described as a *comprador* relationship. The term dates back to the European colonial era, when those who arrived in Africa or Asia seeking to make their fortune discovered that they needed an intermediary, a local person who could help guide them through the intricacies of a strange culture, who could, through language and enterprise, bridge the gap so that business could be done. It is considered a pejorative term to many, but I apply it here free from judgment. As an ex-Viet Minh, Trong had done the unusual, quite obviously switched sides, and was not afraid to demonstrate his new allegiance. In time, Nguyen van Trong began to symbolize for me all those Vietnamese who had, for their individual reasons, bought into what we were trying to do and were doing their part to establish something called the Republic of Viet Nam. I do not include in this group those who did so purely—or even largely—for personal profit, although there were many of them. Only a few put everything on the line, and Trong had clearly done so, not only his own life but also those of his wife, son, and daughter. I suspected that even his bosses at the MSW resented his relationships with the Americans and could only imagine what the other side thought of him now. He remained after I left, of course, and I never learned anything about what happened after that, particularly in the final collapse of 1975, but I strongly suspect that he lacked high enough connections to get out, as did so many others.

I didn't inherit George's motorcycle. I purchased it. It was a Suzuki X6 Hustler, a twin cylinder bike of 250cc. It did not take long to realize that I now had the fastest bike in Saigon. There were uncounted numbers of smoky 50cc and 90cc Japanese bikes on the streets, but only I had something bigger, or at least it seemed. The Vietnamese National Police (*Quan Canh*) did have a few motorcycle cops on the streets of Saigon, driving, of all things, Harley Davidsons. Here was America transplanted, regardless of suitability. Only large Vietnamese could handle those monsters, and even they looked woefully inadequate to the machine they were riding. Besides, their Harleys couldn't get off the line like mine could. Mind you, I didn't mess with the National Police, known by most Americans as the "White Mice." It was unlikely that they would do anything to an American, but their reputation made me wary of ever being hauled off to a police station. I would probably pay only with my wallet, but every American viewed the "QC" (the letters on their helmets) with contempt, full of stories about their corruption and lack of interest in enforcing the law.

The National Police were yet another relic of the French whose presence and influence we accepted because, from a distance, it appeared that they were equipped to offer what Americans desire most: "stability." By the time of the French defeat, southern Viet Nam had become the residence of three separate private "armies," although they hardly represented conventional military structures. Two were based in religion, the Buddhist sects of the Cao Dai and the Hoa Hao. The third was the Binh Xuyen, which was quite different, a gangster organization that derived its income from its control of the drug and prostitution trades in Saigon. When the Republic of Viet Nam was establishing itself, one of its first actions was to legitimize the Binh Xuyen by making them the police. This only formalized an arrangement already achieved by the French, but the lesson was clear.

Amid all this good fortune, I had still come to Saigon to work, and did so, gradually learning my way through the CORDS bureaucracy and Saigon traffic, both of which operated under their respective sets of rules, many of which were quite flexible. One welcoming gesture was a notice that I had been promoted to FSR/L-7, a nice boost in pay that still kept me the lowest ranking member of the WVD staff, although at least tied with a few. I had been sent to Lam Dong for a specific—and imminent—purpose. My assignment to the Saigon WVD was recognition that my purpose in Lam Dong had achieved as much as it was going to. The timing of my transfer, however, was entirely due to a slot opening up with George Korn's departure. I had just had to remain in Lam Dong until that happened. Once I arrived, I was not assigned as a backup/contact for a specific region, as four members of the WVD staff were. Their job was to specialize in that region, its problems and its personnel. I was, at first, assigned to various specific projects, one after another, according to their priority.

Roofing Sheets and Bulgur Wheat

We refugee advisors had our own products for distribution just to refugees, and we processed them both through the MSW or CORDS warehouse and transportation system. The most prized commodity among those under our control were sheets of corrugated steel, approximately 4 by 8 feet, stamped in a small wave pattern to keep them from creasing. We always referred to them as "roofing sheets," although they often served as walls as well as a great many other location-specific functions. These ubiquitous items became my first assignment when Roy asked me to "get a handle on the roofing situation." The problem, simply stated, was that no one at WVD knew just how many roofing sheets we had in country and where they were. Roofing sheets were unlike other commodities in that some passed through the GVN warehouse and distribution system. Some were kept in CORDS warehouses, the central one just outside Saigon, plus such regional accumulations as the CORDS officials in each had been able to arrange. I would have no access to any information about the GVN stocks that anyone considered reliable, so my purview was limited to those in U.S. hands. That proved to be difficult enough.

The problem with roofing sheets was primarily that of attitude on the part of other Americans. We were supposed to all be on the same side, from Saigon to the provinces, but you wouldn't know it from the persistent lack of meaningful communication between and among CORDS officials in Saigon, the regional headquarters, and the provinces. The usual response to any request for information from WVD Saigon to a Regional was, "Don't waste our time with these stupid requests! You don't know the situation up here!" I could easily sympathize with this attitude. I had developed it during my time in Bao Loc (particularly about those people who wanted to visit and be briefed about my project) and had been vocal about it. Now, as fate would have it, I was on the other side and painfully aware of the irony. I was more than sympathetic, but I had to do the job I was assigned to do, just as they did.

I Corps was the farthest away, by far the most independent, and its refugee regional headquarters was just plain contentious on most subjects. They dealt with the Refugee Division's request to send me up to examine their roofing sheets quite succinctly: "Don't send anybody up here. We can count as well as you can, and we'll tell you how many roofing sheets we have." That may not be an exact recounting of their words, but it's pretty close. In fact, I never flew up to Da Nang during my entire two years in country, despite my desire to return and see how things had changed since my departure in 1967. I Corps did, eventually (I had to prod them a couple of times), send me some numbers I could use. I had no idea as to their accuracy. I had developed a good relationship with Matt McClellan, the refugee chief for II Corps while in his domain, but he didn't want me back to count roofing sheets any more than I Corps did. He was just more polite about it. He too reported back to us in Saigon but did it rather more quickly. IV Corps was much the same, with a reasonably polite reception and an equally reasonable time frame to get me the information. III Corps was different, but then again III Corps was different in just about every way. This was the natural result of its being the group of provinces surrounding Saigon. These provinces varied considerably in geography and population, from waterlogged Gia Dinh, which was the donut to Saigon's hole and whose population was swollen with refugees and government workers, to Phuoc Long, mountainous, forested, sparsely populated, and adjacent to the Cambodian border. III Corps headquarters was in Bien Hoa, which was not only close to Saigon but also was connected to it by an asphalted four-lane highway, certainly the most heavily traveled road in all of Viet Nam. III Corps advisors stationed in Bien Hoa were required to live there, at least formally, although the flesh pots of Saigon were never far away. More relevant to me was the fact that MACV/CORDS operated a number of quite large warehouses in the area, at Tu Duc. These held the commodities and other items in the supply chain at the national level before they were shipped out to the multitude of locations. There was really no point in III Corps having separate warehouses that would be no closer than the national ones, so its Refugee Division drew its roofing sheets directly from the national ones. This meant that I could—and, in fact, had to—visit each warehouse that housed roofing sheets, locate, and count for myself how many were where. Thus my initial familiarity with Saigon focused on how to get into and out of town. I visited several warehouses during this period, finding and counting the piles of roofing sheets and making it a point to strike up a relationship with the American warehouse advisors who were attempting to structure the more or less constant chaos that surrounded them. This would pay off later, at the very end of my time in country.

I prepared my report upon receiving the last of the promised regional summaries (from I Corps, of course) and duly submitted it to Roy. He was impressed enough to mention my work on this initial project in the first personnel evaluation report (PER) he would write for me. I was able to follow up from time to time only on the national/III Corps warehouses, so my report's overall usefulness faded rather quickly. Of course, that was true of just about everything written about conditions in South Viet Nam.

Food supplies were a very different situation. One day the Refugee Division had a visit from an army brigadier general who apparently held a high position at MACV headquarters (army titles and acronyms made it difficult to determine just who supervised whom). I'll just call him "General Jackass." He was tall, broad-shouldered, loud, and opinionated. He had been looking over the commodities portion of the CORDS operation and had come to us specifically to learn why there was so much Food for Peace for sale in virtually every local market. We delicately explained to him that it was because the Vietnamese would not eat the stuff, the bulgur wheat in particular. He huffed and puffed about people not understanding when they had a good thing going (actually, they did) and then said he would like a bag of the bulgur wheat. He declared that he would see that it was "served in the MACV General Officers' mess." It was an offhand comment actually, not a direct command, but I simply could not pass up the opportunity. A few days later I obtained a bag of bulgur from the MSW (I didn't explain to them why I wanted it) and loaded it in the back of my green jeep. One of my colleagues saw it there and asked what was up. I reminded him of General Jackass's request for bulgur, and said I was going to take a bag to his office at MACV. He laughed and asked to go along, saying he "wasn't going to miss this for the world." Together we drove out to "Pentagon East," where we parked near the main entrance. I casually hoisted the bag over my right shoulder and was about to head to the security gate when my colleague said, "Mike, that bag is leaking!" I put it down, looked, and sure enough, there was a small hole in one corner of the bag. It just wasn't big enough. I enlarged it slightly with my finger, so we would leave something more resembling a trail, then shouldered the bag once more and walked to the gate. A very surprised security guard looked skeptical, but as we were American civilians and not armed he let us through. I proudly walked through the front door of "Pentagon East," went down the hall to the right, and came to the general's office rather quickly. Given the size of that building, that meant that he may have actually held an important position in MACV.

The security guard's surprise was nothing compared to the look we got from the general's secretary when we walked into his office. She recovered to politely ask why we were there, and I replied that I was responding to the general's request for a bag of bulgur wheat to serve in the general officers' mess. She noticed the leak, and after I gave her a raised eyebrow of "I know," she called the general on the intercom to announce our presence while trying not to break out laughing. She was a professional, so the smile was gone by the time he emerged from his office. She continued to suppress it as I, all business, introduced myself and said I was delivering the bag of bulgur wheat he had asked for. He was clearly taken aback, but long service in the army had taught him the value of playing it straight, so he thanked us and had me put the bag down in a corner. We then politely exited and managed to restrain ourselves until we were safely down the hall corridor, when we finally gave way to hoots of laughter. I never heard of any bulgur wheat recipes being served at the MACV general officers' mess.

"Congressionals" and Other Requests

As much as we at WVD tried to be proactive—communicating with the regional headquarters and trying to anticipate needs—a great deal of the Refugee Division staff's time was purely reactive, as "situations" just seemed to keep happening. Most of this was to aid war victims who had just been generated, a regular occurrence during the active phase of the American military involvement but definitely happening much less now. Most of our reactive work had two sources: provincial/district CORDS officers talking outside the chain of command and individuals (almost always military) who had just returned to "The World" and told someone about a problem they had witnessed. Both of these tended to be sad tales of the treatment of Montagnards, about whom the GVN cared less than little. Several heart-rending stories came to us of small groups displaced for various reasons and left in exposed locations, lacking basic shelter, food, and water. We had only sympathy with those who had initiated these inquiries, particularly if they had been on site and had witnessed what was happening. The timing was often late, as a U.S. soldier might tell the story upon arrival at home, generating local outrage, but we looked into every incident that was reported to us.

Those from CORDS officers often came to us personally because many PSAs wanted no "bad news" emerging from their bailiwicks. They did, at least, come to us comparatively quickly, and we could respond with some hope of actually accomplishing something. Unfortunately, during our follow-up we often had difficulty answering the question—which was always asked by the PSA/DPDA—about where our information came from. By contrast, those originating with returned military personnel took far too much time to reach us. But these late-arriving complaints always had the higher priority because they usually came to us in the form of "Congressionals." That meant that despite their origin, they had been transmitted to CORDS Saigon via a request from member of Congress. These Congressionals always received the highest priority. Each such letter was stapled to a large piece of cardboard that had "Action Required" printed prominently across the top. This assembly would be given to a staff member to research and prepare a response and a date to by which to produce it. Some inquiries were less welcome than others, and most of those emerged from the Senate Select Committee on Indochina Refugees, chaired by Senator Ted Kennedy. We saw these repeated missives as politically motivated because they really couldn't be addressed, but they were given the highest priority nonetheless. They were rather more than just Congressionals, and the priority they received was the highest of the high and given the swiftest turnaround response.

The problem, at least as I saw it, was that each written response to a complaint about refugees, regardless of its source, had to conform to a rigid pattern. We were required to craft a response that fell within strict guidelines (which were verbal and never written down). Under no circumstances was a response to leave WVD without its being properly phrased to make it clear that our response was alleviating the problem. Each could leave only if signed by either Swart or Hearns, which assured that nothing did unless it conformed to "The Program." While I may or may not have objected to this aspect, depending on whether the problem was actually being alleviated, I always objected to what I so often observed, that the process of reply was actually a process of watering down the response, even to the extent of lightly phrasing—if not removing altogether—any wording that demonstrated the seriousness of the original problem. I remember one such notice—among far too many—we received of a group of Montagnards whose small village had been destroyed (for private, commercial, and not war-related reasons) and who had been forced to live without shelter and food for some time, with several deaths resulting. I was charged with the response to this and drafted the initial reply. It was returned quickly, and a back-and-forth drafting war between the director's office and I resulted. In the end, the formal response managed to not even once employ the word "death." These small incidents, which were cover-ups but in context pretty damn minor ones, did slowly accumulate on me, contributing to a steadily decreasing feeling of job satisfaction.

One member of the WVD staff felt considerably angrier than I did about our efforts to aid war victims, as I would learn only after the fact. Isaac Ross was another one who had quarreled with his provincial CORDS team, had been returned to Saigon, and was assigned to WVD. He spent only a couple of months with us, basically killing time, and I was not his supervisor. Some time after he left, Norman Hearns called Roy and me into his office and began by asking us, "How well did you know Isaac Ross?" Both of us had to admit to "not much." My one memory of him was that he seemed to spend a lot of time at the copying machine. It turns out he did just that, making copies of every document he could find that cast doubt on our work—and they weren't hard to find. Upon arrival in the States, he proceeded directly to Washington, D.C., and turned over his copies to the Kennedy committee. USAID was not pleased and let us know by cable. We heard nothing further from USAID, but we certainly did from the Kennedy committee.

The "Times Square Hooker"

Getting our responses typed in a final form was a constant headache at WVD, and at every other Directorate, as local talk had it. Most of the "secretaries" were Vietnamese and worked for the division in general, not for individuals. They had a hard time producing an acceptably typed report, as might be expected in their second (or third) language. They also had the only typewriters, so I could not return to my old habits of typing reports myself, although I often wished to. Had I done so, I know, I would have been admonished, because *everybody* had their slot to fill. There were two American female "secretaries" in the upper floor of USAID II, working in the offices of some unremembered higher-ups. Neither ever appeared to be very busy but both flatly refused to take on work from our office or any other. We all believed, partly on the basis of their privileged exemption from sharing the workload but primarily on the basis of their physical appearance, that their real work was done after hours and rarely in a chair. One was short and somewhat heavy, the other was, by contrast, tall and statuesque. I rarely saw the shorter one, but the tall one always seemed to be walking by, going somewhere with nothing in her hands but drawing everyone's attention anyway. You always knew she was coming by the ringing sound her heels made on the tile floors. And they were *some* heels, four to five inches, with elaborate foot straps. They didn't get much attention, however, as her attire above them was invariably short, tight skirts with dark stockings on her noticeably long legs, and tight, diaphanous blouses. She always dressed, in the words of one of my WVD associates (a woman, by the way), "like a Times Square hooker." Heavily made up, she wore her hair high in a rigid, bouffant style, but she was getting a little long in the tooth for the sex kitten role. The body had held up well, a fact that was prominently displayed, but the wear and tear had begun to show on her face despite obvious attempts to hide the years. General opinion held that she was an old warhorse who had been ridden into many battles, but none of us ever knew for sure, until I ran into Fred Gymball once again, in Saigon.

It was purely coincidental; he was in town to catch up with some personnel items regarding his family in Australia, and I bumped into him at the little CORDS II café. We sat down, and he began to speak of things back in Lam Dong. There had been much change, as Advisory Team #38 had been drastically reduced in size, with the military component mostly gone, causing the MACV compound to be closed. The new PSA, a lieutenant colonel (signaling the reduced size of his command), now lived in the CORDS compound. Then Fred's rendition of events paused in mid-sentence as The Hooker ankled by. His eyes widened in astonishment, and he, with open mouth, silently watched her pass by and walk out of sight. It was the one and only time I ever saw Fred Gymball at a loss for words. It even took him a few minutes to speak to me again. "Damn!" he finally spoke. "I don't believe it. I haven't seen her in years." Then he chuckled. "Last time was in Athens [Greece], back in 1947. We were all at some off-limits apartment having a big party when the MPs came busting in. It was chaos. Last time I saw her she was being helped out a window by three men." Talk about a career in international relations!

Suoi Nghe

Roy called me in one day and told me he was sending me on a temporary duty (TDY) assignment to Phuoc Tuy Province, in III Corps, to advise and report on a major refugee resettlement project about to get underway. I was the only member of the current Refugee Division Saigon staff with experience in such large resettlements, and the Phuoc Tuy Advisory Team had no refugee advisor, so I was sent. This was a major project; the refugees had been generated in Quang Tri Province (perhaps more than once) at the northern tip of South Viet Nam. The security situation was simply not going to get any better with the Americans almost gone, so it had been decided that they would be resettled in Phuoc Tuy. The new refugee settlement was called Suoi Nghe. I was to be there only during the initial resettlement phase, and so it turned out. I was there for less than three weeks. Phuoc Tuy Province was in southeastern III Corps, with a coastline and at its tip the old seaside resort of Vung Tau, by that time the new military port of the same name. Despite its being in III Corps and quite close, with a perfectly acceptable—and heavily travelled—road between it and Saigon, I was required by protocol to fly via Air America. I landed at the airstrip at the provincial capital of Ba Ria. It was there that I photographed the "Arrivals Anytime, Departures Immediately" sign that appears in the photos here, but the sign expressed the reality of virtually every provincial and district airstrip in South Viet Nam.

The flight was my introduction to a unique type of airplane in the Air America fleet, the Pilatus Porter. It was used as the Regional Courier on these short III Corps flights, and all through IV Corps in the delta. Anywhere the flight times were short and the airstrips shorter you would find a Porter. They were tail-draggers, like every Air America plane I flew after that first Volpar flight in 1967, but at that point all resemblance ended. The Porter was a new design, originating in the Alps, where short takeoff and landing (STOL) capability is the primary design component. Its large, high wing and light metal construction gave it a slow takeoff and landing speed, but the key to its performance was its engine. This was no 1930s-era radial, but a modern turbine, in a decidedly pointed nose. A pilot later explained to me (in a simplified manner, I always supposed) that he didn't use a throttle to control the plane's speed, that he just brought it up to the operating range and left it there. When he needed to increase or decrease his plane's speed, he had only to adjust the pitch of

Sign at the Ba Ria airstrip, Phuoc Tuy Province, 1972.

the propeller. Porters could "land on a dime and give you a nickel change." I would fly them on a semiregular basis during my trips in IV Corps, and it never ceased to amaze me how many Vietnamese could be loaded into such a small plane and still take off quickly.

The unusual thing about Phuoc Tuy's CORDS Advisory Team was that the PSA was a civilian, an FSO, while the DPSA was military, a lieutenant colonel. Such an arrangement was striking because Phuoc Tuy had historically been quite insecure. It had become the main location for the military contingent sent by Australia, but they were also withdrawing by this time. I met only one Australian soldier during my time there, an officer I met on my first day. His first move, after the handshake, was to pull a box of opals out of his pocket and try to sell me some. I declined.

I did as I was directed at Saigon, to the maximum extent possible. There was no time to establish anything like a counterpart relationship, so the Vietnamese simply assumed I was there to keep watch and report back to Saigon. So too did the CORDS team, if to a lesser extent, and both were right. There would be no actual function for me to perform unless something went wrong in the initial reception and distribution phases, and nothing did. That and the absence of any real access to the MSW

The Pilatus Porter (1971) was perfect for the plethora of short, unimproved dirt airstrips in Viet Nam.

provincial representative combined to make this task even more about reporting than my previous one. Much counting of roofing sheets, buildings constructed, and the like constituted my reports, verbal to the advisory team and in writing to WVD. What was becoming a repetitive question arose again in my mind: *What am I doing here?*

Evidence that the Suoi Nghe project was a very big deal arrived once the refugees had been settled in their tents and given their initial rations. The GVN/ARVN organized an official dedication ceremony. The provincial government had gone all out to prepare a large area for a public reception. A makeshift grandstand had been constructed in an open field and care taken to keep people in some semblance of order (in contrast to the usual practice). On the appointed day, the audience of refugees dutifully arrived, having been herded from their new homes. Local GVN officials— the province chief and some of his staff, accompanied by the much smaller contingent of American advisors—were given places of honor. I declined and did my futile best to blend into the crowd. Photos taken at that event (I can't remember by whom) testify how difficult that was, as I had grown the beard I wear to this day.

Once everyone was in place we saw three helicopters approach from

Young refugee arriving at Phuoc Tuy from Quang Tri Province, 1972.

near tree-top level, a Huey flanked by two Cobras.[1] They simultaneously throttled back from a high speed, executed a tight right-hand turn and landed closely together, all in less time than it takes to read this sentence. Quite impressive, as it was meant to be. GVN prime minister—and, of course, ARVN general—Khiem stepped out, closely escorted even here by some zealous bodyguards. Prime Minister Khiem was well known as "Thieu's Toady" and was often trotted out for such functions. There followed the more or less standard GVN ceremony, versions of which I had witnessed before, from the most humble to this one, clearly the highest level I witnessed. The ceremony did equally well on the American side. Major General Fred Weyand, at that point still deputy to COMUSMACV General Abrams but who would succeed him shortly, was there. His part in the ceremony included handing out a ceremonial packet to some stunned and highly nervous refugees. I couldn't help but think how the mighty had fallen: the soon-to-be COMUSMACV, with virtually no combat troops to command, reduced to handing out blankets to refugees at a

GVN ceremony. When I returned to Saigon, I knew that the GVN had again done its job of initially settling refugees. My major questions about the project were the usual ones: will they receive arable land to till, and WHAT ABOUT SECURITY? Both subjects were, of course, way out of my jurisdiction, so I stifled any skeptical questions in speaking to the MSW representative. However, I did voice them to both the PSA and the DPSA. By the time I left country, nothing yet had gone wrong, at least nothing important enough to appear in *Stars and Stripes*.

During my free time in province, I had made it a point to drive around as much as possible, particularly along the coastline and toward Vung Tau. One road made its way along the coast, where pristine beaches appeared, one after another. Every kilometer or so I would see, perched on a pinnacle overlooking the sea, what had formerly been a beautiful seaside house, undoubtedly French-owned. Each was abandoned and much shot up, with all glass long gone and often some substantial portions of the structure itself missing. It was sad and recalled a more peaceable time. Of course, no VC would ever dream of getting holed up in such a prominent and indefensible position, so all the damage to the houses had come from ARVN target practice, i.e., sheer wanton destruction.

Much more etched in my mind were trips down another road—not a major one, but asphalt nonetheless—that I would often make in the morning. There were no buildings, and I turned off before I learned where the road actually led. But each time I drove down that road I would pass two long lines of men, one on each side, all walking in the same direction. They were dressed identically, in tan shirts and shorts, each with a floppy, wide-brimmed hat on his head. They were all young, grinning and smiling as they walked along, despite the rifle each carried. They were not Viet-namese. I inquired at the advisory team, and learned that what I suspected was true. They were Cambodians, young "recruits" for Lon Nol's army being trained somewhere near Vung Tau. That's all I ever learned. I saw these men only a few times, but of all the images of Viet Nam I retain, the memory of two lines of smiling young men, so cheerfully unaware of the fate that awaited them, is by far the most prominent, seared into my brain.

My work in Phuoc Tuy got me in trouble with Mr. Swart and led to only the second one-on-one meeting we were to have. He was quite unhappy with my performance and told me so. What was less clear was just exactly what he based this on. It seems that he had objected to the entire project in the first place and during my stay had periodically sent short directives to me specifying what I was to make sure was done. Unfortunately, lacking any form of leverage, either with the GVN or the local CORDS advisory team, and increasingly seeing that his directives were not based on the real situation, I made no attempt to enforce them, as indeed I could not. The PSA treated me well, but had I used my back channel to Saigon and not cleared everything through him first my stay would have been considerably shorter than it was. My post-assignment debriefing with Mr. Swart (I am gilding the lily here, as he didn't want to know what had really happened and why) did not go well.

Our director may have lost confidence in me, but Roy Fontall had not. Shortly after my return to Saigon, he appointed me deputy chief of the Refugee Division, first de facto, and then formally (at least within WVD). This was rather less than it sounds, as it meant only daily supervision of the staff's activities, particularly requests received and responses undertaken. I made nothing resembling a major decision; I just took some of the day-to-day activities off of Roy's shoulders. Later, as the position became formal (meaning I would have to write personnel evaluation reports for some of the staff), problems arose. I had good working relationships with the other members of the staff, but I did not outrank them. This was a sore point in any bureaucracy, and it is a credit to the WVD staff—and their expectations of no further USAID career—that we managed several ways to get around that problem.

The primary reason I relieved Roy of the day-to-day staff supervision was to allow him to spend more time with Dr. Phan Quang Dan. Dr. Dan at this time was the GVN Minister of State, which sounds impressive, but in the GVN structure meant not only did he have no portfolio he also had no power. He was a favorite of the Americans and probably the national figure closest to what we would have liked to see in the presidency. He had played a part in Vietnamese politics back to the days of Emperor Bao Dai but always as the dissenter and thus viewed with varying degrees of suspicion by all sides. He had been one of the few who had spoken out against Diem back when it was dangerous to do so and had suffered the consequences. But that was before the military had assumed total control under the guise of democracy and delegated the civilians to irrelevance. By this time, Dr. Dan had assumed responsibility for several social welfare programs, refugees prominent among them. He had big ideas and Roy was inspired by them, constantly speaking to us of what Dr. Dan wanted to do.

Dr. Dan was an energetic man and traveled frequently. His real function out in the provinces seemed to be morale-raising visits, always carefully choreographed. But whenever he wanted to make such a trip, the GVN never provided a plane. Dr. Dan would get Roy to arrange a charter with Air America, because while Dr. Dan may have been the GVN Minister of State, he couldn't request an Air America plane. On two of those occasions, Roy begged off at the last minute and sent me instead, as an American had to be on the flight.

The first was a classic dog and pony show, with Dr. Dan, after a formal welcoming ceremony, walking through a village smiling and waving to the people who had obediently gathered to greet him, then flying elsewhere and repeating the whole scene. I was particularly amused by the PF soldiers who preceded him on these walks through the delta villages. They would be about twenty feet in front of him and quite ostentatiously wading into bushes, pointing their rifles, etc., in search of any VC who might have decided to wait until he was surrounded by scores of people before mounting his assault. The second trip was something very different. It took place late in my tour, and I discuss it later.

The Hard Life in a War Zone

When Barbara first came to Saigon (and I was still in Bao Loc), she worked as secretary to the director of operations of Control Data, Saigon. Within a few months, she was transferred to work with one of the private contractors hired to do research about the GVN land reform program. This was all under the direction of Howard Brush, PhD, and Barbara became his administrative assistant. We still have several photos of Howard Brush, most taken at parties. He is mugging shamelessly in every one of them. He wasn't drunk, that was just his public persona. Those who saw only that side of him missed the core of Howard Brush. He was a thorough professional who ran his operation in an equally professional manner. His job was to determine the attitudes of the Vietnamese peasants affected by the GVN land reform program, "Land to the Tiller" (*Nguoi Cay Ca Rung*). For this he trained a group of Americans and Vietnamese in the subjectively neutral techniques of information collection by interview. They would proceed about the villages and hamlets affected by the program residents, repeating the interviews with more and more people. They would then bring back data, organize it at the office, and interpret it under Dr. Brush's direction. Barbara would type the final work, which would be many pages long. I thought highly of the program and of Dr. Brush but couldn't help reflecting that this was all "too little, too late."

Once settled in Saigon, Barbara and I began to explore both its daytime attractions and its opportunities for after-hours entertainment. Now that I was in the south of Viet Nam, I could understand a great deal more of what was said in Vietnamese near me, something I had experienced great trouble with in Lam Dong. The regional differences did make a considerable difference, and I had only partially adjusted to the northern dialect before I found myself back with people speaking the southern one. Things were easier from then on, precisely when I didn't need them to be. They were also more fun.

Downtown Saigon

Saigon was technically a seaport, but a slow, torturous journey along the Saigon River was required to make the trip to and from the South China Sea. The Americans had realized its inadequacy early on and had built an entirely new, modern, and much larger port closer to the ocean. They named it, uninspiringly, "New Port." This was but one of the enormous number of construction projects undertaken throughout the country in support of the U.S. military effort.[2] The work was done through a consortium of companies known as RMK-BRJ. This stood for Raymond, Morrison-Knudsen, Brown & Root, and J.A. Jones Construction Co. This was a profitable effort, to say the least. The inclusion of Brown & Root was a payback from President Lyndon Johnson, whose career had been lavishly financed by the company from the time he was Congressman Lyndon Johnson. This situation greatly reduced the importance of Saigon's waterfront, but its French-era downtown area was nearby and bustling. Downtown Saigon back then emanated from the intersection of Tu Do ["Freedom"] and Le Loi streets. The major buildings nearby testified to the French presence, particularly the Continental Palace, where sitting in the open-air bar downstairs evoked thoughts of Graham Greene and a time when Americans were quiet. Several of the old French buildings were being used by the Americans, including the Rex Hotel, where I had spent my first night in Viet Nam in 1967. I had been closer to the core of things than I had realized at the time.

The structure the French had built as an opera house, at the intersection of those two streets, was the focal point of the area. It had been built in 1900, in the "Third Republic" style. Since 1955 it had housed the Assembly of the Republic of Viet Nam, its parliament. The building in its former life had hosted internationally known classics, often tragedies, but during the American time it offered only locally produced dramas, composed of equal parts tragedy and farce. The farce was easily visible by all; the tragedy was as hidden as was possible. Easily the most visible feature of downtown was not a building but a statue. It was the ARVN monument, a large rendering of two soldiers charging indomitably forward toward their foes. The fact that the two appeared to be charging the building housing the National Assembly, a fact made note of by everyone, was not believed to be just a coincidence.

We both loved walking around Saigon and did so on weekends, although we usually avoided the middle of the day, of course. A short trip by jeep took us downtown, where we parked in the nearest American-patrolled lot and then went exploring, walking around the city streets. Most of all we loved walking among the open-air markets that seemed to be everywhere along the sidewalks. There were many subjects I lacked the Vietnamese vocabulary to discuss but going to market is survival level in every language, and by this point it was simple. It was also fun because I could get past the numbers for some give-and-take with the vendors while haggling over price. I could add a few twists to those of most Americans trying not to get badly taken at a market. My favorite protestation was to claim that I was only a "poor American" (*My ngheo*) and couldn't afford such a high price. This invariably drew guffaws from all within earshot. The average Vietnamese could not even grasp the concept of a "poor American." All this meant we paid better prices, but we were getting taken anyway, just by less, and that was the victory.

We were quite the objects of view during these walks, particularly the blonde American woman. Many admired Barbara from a distance, but I was always the one approached and touched. Time after time, a Vietnamese—always a man, by the way—would come up from behind me and reach out, grabbing the hair at my wrists and tugging sharply. The phenomenon my hairy wrists and arms presented in a short-sleeve shirt never ceased to draw someone's approach. It didn't take me long to realize that my wrists were simply more evidence that Americans were big, hairy beasts, crude and clumsy, however immensely powerful we were in groups. In my defense, I can only say that at least my behavior in public did not contribute to this belief. This put me in a distinct minority among those Americans you saw walking around Saigon, particularly those who wore uniforms. Saigon was a kaleidoscope of sights and sounds, and a joy to just experience. This did require ignoring the omnipresent sandbag bunkers and men in uniform carrying guns, but it could be done with determination.

A young Vietnamese woman in a diaphanous white *ao dai* is the very definition of grace; she seems to just glide along the ground. One girl walking by, or a group of them, is a scene of kinetic grace. How they managed to keep their clothing so white in a land of dirt, rain, and mud was a mystery to every American, myself most definitely included. During my time in Saigon I did on occasion encounter an American woman wearing an *ao dai*, usually at a party. None could quite pull it off, in the fashion sense. Vietnamese women seemed to carry grace with them, as an unconscious adornment, regardless of their situation or position. It was most apparent when they were walking or pedaling a bicycle, but they even demonstrated their innate grace on that staple of city traffic, the light Japanese motorcycles, the step-through Honda 50ccs with their plastic front fairing and the more conventional 90cc models with a straddle gas tank, from Honda, Yamaha, and Kawasaki. I saw countless such vehicles in Saigon and other urban centers. A great many of them carried women; a few were drivers, but only on the step-through models. A great many more rode on the rear of the motorcycles that weaved in and out of traffic. But I never, repeat NEVER, saw a Vietnamese woman straddling a motorcycle, whether driving one or as a passenger. They always sat sidesaddle on the rear, calm and composed and leaning left or right as their drivers needed to facilitate their rapid passage through the barely organized chaos of urban traffic, often holding packages or children. Quite a sight.

Working women, usually older, wore the more utilitarian version of the ao dai, with the front and rear panels cut to just below the waist. When I say working women, I mean physical labor. They were a ubiquitous sight, working as coolies, diggers, stevedores, or a thousand other of the physical tasks Vietnamese women had been forced to assume. Women had found it necessary to become the laboring class because one consequence of the draft was to leave virtually no men left to perform the various tasks of a civilian laborer. But young male civilian men did exist. Known as "Saigon cowboys," they had purchased their exemption from the military or were part of some other scam. You never saw them actually doing any work. You did frequently see them on motorcycles, clearly enjoying their favored and protected status. Twice I had my sunglasses ripped off my face while I was out riding my bicycle, each time by the rider on the back of a motorcycle, who would then wave them at me as the vehicle disappeared down the street. But once I had my 250cc Suzuki, I substituted it for the bicycle and I assure you that didn't happen again. They could still have snuck up on me from the rear and grabbed my glasses, but they couldn't have gotten away from me and they knew it. I had the fastest bike in Saigon.

Walking around and market shopping were common enough pursuits, but Barbara and I found a less common one: seeing a movie at one of the many small theatres in town. These were small, narrow, and by no means the usual haunt of Americans. Let's just say that we were glad that everything was always dark when we found our seats, during the movie, and afterward. I developed something of a taste for the movies shown in these theaters, those produced in Hong Kong by Run Run Shaw. They were all set in old China and were in Chinese with English subtitles (not well rendered). They explored old Chinese folk tales, but the line between fantasy and reality was nonexistent, which added to the fun. Most we saw were stories of warriors, including some rather improbable ones. My favorite was the beggar woman who was an expert with the sword, dispatching a small army of enemies during the film's short run, despite the fact that she was blind.

Still, American movies were our favorites, and they were available just out of town at the MACV complex. There were two theaters and both showed first-run movies. One was a conventional type, with nice seats, while the other was an outdoor site. It was very lacking in amenities, but seeing a movie under the stars (in at least slightly more bearable evening weather) had its attractions too. We did both.

And then there was the food. To say that I was overwhelmed with new menu choices would be an understatement. Much of this was my fault, or rather that of my upbringing, during which Kraft macaroni and cheese was the favored staple. Upon leaving my mother's care, I spent four years largely eating at a college cafeteria and not exactly expanding my dietary choices. I thus arrived in Viet Nam a total naïf in the world of cuisine. That didn't matter for almost a year, as I ate at the advisory team mess. This was not only American food, it was also basic, meat-and-potatoes American food, better than I had grown up eating but limited in its aspirations.

Upon transferring to Saigon, I was quite literally surrounded by "foreign" restaurants, and by this I mean French more than Asian. We always carried the typical attitude of Americans toward the French in Viet Nam, with rather more intensity and a great deal more justification than most, but we all admitted to a man (and woman) that they had exerted a beneficial effect on Vietnamese cuisine, if somewhat indirectly, i.e., bread. French cuisine was a complete mystery to me, and given my total lack of preparation I could not tell whether they offered haute French cuisine or something a level or more below. But it sure didn't matter. I probably didn't order my first salad at a Saigon restaurant, but they actually began to enter my regular diet, where before they had hardly appeared at all. A particularly clear memory is that of first seeing baked Alaska, prepared and served at a nearby table.

Post Exchange, Commissary and PACEX

I didn't make a great deal of money, despite my promotion to FSR/L-7 and the pay boost we all received for being in country. Barbara didn't either, but together we learned that great economic truth: it's not what you earn, it's what you spend. We paid no rent, and with the free gas my vehicle expenses were limited to maintenance, so the big two were taken care of. Best of all, we purchased life's necessities at artificially low prices at the PX and commissary. Both institutions were located at Tan Son Nhut Airbase, and they were sights to behold. A great many American military men were stationed nearby, and besides, there was no competition from any other store. A gourmet might have questioned the variety of offerings in the commissary, but no one could argue with the prices. Both the PX and the commissary are well-deserved U.S. Army traditions. Their prices are kept traditionally low, as soldiers don't make much money. We continued to eat American style and so bought most of our food at the commissary.

The PX at Tan Son Nhut airbase was incredible. I had only limited experience with the PX and commissary at Sangley Point, in the Philippines, but I bet this was one of the largest ever, and it offered an enormous variety of enticements at remarkably low prices.[3] The PX and the commissary were the most understandable components of the futile U.S. effort to keep American money from flowing into the local economy. The problem that a wide array of items at low prices tried to alleviate was a real one, one that had, in fact, overwhelmed the country, its economy, and its people, particularly regarding their ethics and morals. Wherever I went throughout the country, I saw evidence of the obscene economic impact our presence had resulted in. Nowhere was this more evident than in Saigon, where whores could earn more money than cabinet ministers (at least honest ones).

We had instituted several other, less defensible, programs to try to soak up some of that money. These accounted for, among other things, the uncounted number of Japanese motorcycles on the streets and the remarkable number of products available in the downtown Saigon markets. It also accounted for the large number of Vietnamese businessmen with the right connections to the ruling military who had made fortunes importing such items under the program. This multitude of good-intentioned efforts may have soaked up some of the loose American money, but it definitely solidified the power, wealth, and influence of the well-connected elites, not to mention that it distorted beyond all recognition the agricultural economy of Viet Nam.

I also believe that one of those programs in the long run caused severe damage to the American economy. This was the Pacific Exchange Program, or PACEX. A huge number of items were marketed through its large, glossy catalog titled with that acronym. Every solider and civilian had access to these catalogs, which were widely distributed. The PACEX catalog was packed with items from jewelry and chinaware to electronics. The message seemed to be "Buy Japanese!" The PACEX catalog showed Americans how they could purchase things of both beauty and utility from Japan. It introduced countless Americans to the products of Mikimoto, Sony, Canon, Panasonic, Hitachi, Pioneer, and a host of others. In the early 1960s, the phrase "made in Japan" was the punch line of a joke. By the end of the decade it had begun to acquire an entirely different meaning. How much of this was due to the many thousands of young American men who had returned to the U.S. in possession of stereo equipment made in Japan and marketed by PACEX? This flow would subside and then end, but by that time how many more men—and some women—would have returned to the U.S. well acquainted with the quality of Japanese products and receptive to buying more when their income warranted it?

The only major exception to the "made in Japan" nature of PACEX items, to my knowledge, was automobiles. U.S. manufacturers offered deals at the Saigon PX through agents who handled a wide variety of things to entice the lonely individual longing for life back in "the world." In early 1972 Barbara and I purchased a Winnebago motorhome—at a substantial discount—through the Chrysler Motors representative at the Saigon PX, arranging to pick one of the new 1973 models at the factory in Forest City, Iowa, that coming September, all done from halfway around the world and with no fuss. The Winnebago would be our biggest purchase, and we passed on the more popular expensive items, such as the admittedly beautiful lacquered inlaid mother of pearl furniture. I did, however, fulfill a dream that would otherwise have not been obtainable: a complete, matched set of left-handed golf clubs. One Saturday, while picking up some groceries and sundries at the PX and commissary at the Tan Son Nhut complex, I stopped by the pro shop purely on impulse. I hadn't appreciated what a stock it had. Wandering around, I spotted just sitting there a complete set of clubs—four woods and all irons except putter and sand wedge. AND THEY WERE LEFT-HANDED CLUBS! Here was my opportunity, and I seized it. I bought the set after checking that they were the right length, etc., added a large golf bag to accommodate them, and walked out the door. I don't remember the price but I assure you it was damn cheap.

I had learned to play (not well) in high school, and had been thinking about golf ever since moving to Saigon. The purchase of a new set of clubs got me to do some real planning. Little got done on the Vietnamese side during the afternoons, particularly in the dry season, and as a consequence we found our afternoons a little slow too. With my new clubs, my solution was to use the slack time to play golf at the Golf Club de Saigon once or twice a week. I could get in a quick nine holes and a light lunch at the club restaurant afterwards, then return to the office and clean up anything that may have occurred during my absence. Only crazy Americans played golf in the noonday sun, so there was no waiting to tee off or for anything else.

The Golf Club de Saigon, a relic of the French occupation, had managed to survive and even thrive, if considerably altered by wartime reality. It lay north of Saigon and right next to the enormous, sprawling mass of buildings and roads that constituted the MACV complex. This had led to great destruction during Tet of '68, when NLF cadres blew holes in the perimeter fence and raced across the course toward MACV headquarters.

Curiously, despite the graphic and bloody evidence of the ease with which the course had been penetrated, the old custom of not clearing a field of fire (or at least vision) had returned. The outside of the new, improved fence along the course's perimeter had been again taken over by squatters and informal merchants, who employed the fence as their back wall and proceeded to construct tin roof huts all along it. Prior to Tet of '68, the VC had used these to place explosives, firearms and ammunition in advance at selected points along the perimeter fence beside the course, directly among the inhabitants, who said nothing, at least to the GVN. The course itself was as flat as a pancake, save where some slight rises for the greens had been constructed. It had clearly been abbreviated and now had fairways crossing one another. The fairways were narrow, as were the roughs. But when you hit into a bunker, you hit into a *bunker*. The sand was in bags, and ARVN soldiers manned each one, desperately trying to remain awake in the midday heat. Women were the only caddies at the Saigon Golf Club. I never ceased to be amazed at how my caddy could carry around a full bag of clubs that was almost as tall as she was and probably weighed at least half as much.

I have mentioned the Saigon heat, but one afternoon as I made my way around the oven that the course had become, I encountered something I had never heard of before or since and did not think was even possible. As I proceeded down a fairway after my tee shot, I noticed ahead of me a large, brown, uneven circle that was slowly expanding. As I approached, I realized that the fairway was actually on fire, its progress marked by the slowly expanding perimeter, despite the almost complete absence of smoke. The fire burned only along the perimeter and was hardly visible until I was right on top of it. My caddy quickly took off her conical hat and ran back and forth to a small stream nearby, filling her hat with water and then pouring it along the fire's perimeter. I took my club-cleaning cloth and began to beat the fire out, working my way around the circle's perimeter. Together we extinguished the fire and then continued our round. My caddy got a special tip that day.

At the restaurant I always confined myself to just soup, with some of that delicious bread. I deliberately avoided what I knew others were doing during this afternoon slow time, which was drink alcohol. It helped that I still retained the distaste for hard liquor I had developed during my time behind the bar at the Cellar Door. Wine was a different story, and Saigon was an excellent place for a neophyte like me to learn about the subject.

I also began a tradition at the Refugee Division of a Friday after-work party, featuring champagne cooled in small trash cans by ice from the snack bar downstairs. The stuff was so damn cheap just wine wouldn't do. I did develop one exception to my distaste for hard liquor, specifically that seductive siren of the tropics, the gin and tonic. The reason was not the gin but the tonic, which was tasty and mixed exquisitely with the gin, adding a distinctive flavor. I was, like everyone else at his first encounter with this liquid, rather taken aback by its blue color. This concern lasted as long as it took me to swallow my first sip. It may have been light blue, but it was delicious. I decided to ignore the question of exactly what made it blue because I really didn't want to know.

I was in Saigon for the Republic of Viet Nam's 1971 "National Day," which, if I remember correctly, was in August. A large parade had been planned through downtown Saigon. Workers spent the days before it marking off the parade route and installing bleachers and crowd direction barriers. There was going to be considerable security, and only GVN employees and their families were invited into the bleachers. I had no invitation, of course, but decided to attend anyway. I was stopped several times as I worked my way through the layers of security, but each time my Vietnamese saw me through. I was friendly and polite and didn't take no for an answer. I approached a group of bleachers along the parade route and climbed up the stairs to the passageway between the rows of benches on each side. This was clearly as far as I should go, so I just sidled close to one side and stood there, trying to look inconspicuous and failing miserably, no doubt.

The GVN/ARVN did put on a good parade. Every form of tank, armored personnel carrier, truck, and jeep passed by, all crewed by smartly turned out members of the armed forces, with seemingly all branches being represented, including women. Even the black pajamas of the RD Cadre groups marching past were clean and carefully pressed. I had tired of this show and was about to leave when I saw coming down the street Great Britain's contribution to the Viet Nam war, a marching band. And not just a band, a Highland bagpipe band in full uniform. So I stayed. I felt great sympathy for them, marching down the street on a scorching Saigon day. Their kilts helped, I'm sure, but each man was also laden down with substantial amounts of fur, including those tall hats, and had to wear knee socks, plus some leather and brass, not to mention carry an instrument. Their appearance delighted the audience; they had never seen anything like this. Huge men in bizarre costumes wearing tall fur hats and skirts! The crowd pointed and tittered, entranced with the sight. As the band was about to come abreast of where I was standing, the drum major twirled his mace, the bass drummer briefly played an intro beat, and the pipers puffed up the bags under their arms. As a long-time fan of bagpipes, I knew what was coming next, but the Vietnamese in the stands around me had no idea. On the signal, the drums beat and the pipes blasted forth with that singular sound that only bagpipes can make.

What followed was the very definition of "the crowd went wild." The grandstands on both sides, a moment before the site of much laughter and pointing, literally erupted. Women shrieked and covered their ears or their children's ears as best they could. Men did the same. Families cowered in groups, huddling together against the aural assault. Many of both sexes jumped to their feet and fled hysterically, holding their ears all the while. I had to press close to the side of the grandstand passageway to avoid being swept along with what quickly became a human tide running away from the sounds. As the initial rush diminished, I looked around at the nearby grandstands and saw that the same thing had happened in them all. All else was in order up and down the parade route, but the nearby stands were in chaos. After the band had marched past, droning, thumping, and wailing its way down the street to wreak further havoc later, the huddled groups near me slowly disbanded and the people still left in the stands tried to compose themselves and their children. Some began to return to the seats they had fled in terror. After things returned to something approaching normal (the parade was still going on), I thought about staying but nothing I might see could top what I had just seen, so I quietly departed and went home.

Day Tripper

These being the salad days of security in Viet Nam, before the NVA made the fundamentally changed nature of the war quite apparent in the spring of 1972, Barbara and I were able to take short day trips out into the countryside. We always drove my jeep, and it never gave me a problem during any of the trips, thanks to Trong's attention. These trips usually had no destination. I merely plotted a roundabout course on local roads, and off we went. It was pleasing to observe an area that seemed to be at peace, pursuing only peacetime objectives. Even the formal military presence was minimal, as we were driving through perhaps the most secure provinces in the country. The roads were abysmal, of course, but the jeep had been designed to handle worse than these and we had no problems. My particular delight was to frequently cross one of the numerous canals and streams that characterized the area. We were occasionally taken across on a motorized, if small, ferry, but often it was an even smaller one, containing our jeep, us, and maybe a person or two more, propelled across the waterway by one or two men pulling on a rope strung from bank to bank.

One trip did have a destination, the Cao Dai temple in Tay Ninh Province, which adjoined the Cambodian border. You had to drive through Hau Nghia Province after leaving the Saigon area. Good security during the daylight hours at that time meant that a visit was a very doable day trip. The ride to the site was not too unpleasant, even in my jeep, and the destination was well worth it. The temple proved to be everything people said it was, an incomprehensible collection of bizarre symbols rendered in plaster and vibrant colors that I can only describe as "Asian Rococo." Even during those war years, tourists were a source of income, with interior balconies available for them to look down into the temple itself and a slew of pamphlets for sale. The Cao Dai had been a political and military force in the period of the French collapse and afterward but had been subdued by the ARVN. Its location astride the corridor between Cambodia and Saigon placed it in harm's way on more than one occasion, yet it had managed to survive unscathed. This meant an understanding with both sides, which the Cao Dai certainly seem to have achieved. I found the religion itself fascinating. It is at the same time both syncretic and pretentious. Its basic doctrine is that the father of the universe (Cao Dai) had communicated with humanity in several ways, including Buddha, Confucius, and Jesus, but the message of each had become corrupted. Then, on Christmas Eve 1925, he identified the Third Time of Redemption to those who would become the first group of Cao Dai "mediums" (disciples is a reasonably close translation), in what was then French Cochin China. His followers continued the process of drawing on disparate cultural traditions; the Cao Dai pantheon of "saints" includes Muhammad, Moses, Victor Hugo, Joan of Arc, and Lenin, as well as several more obscure names.

We saw considerable military activity during the trip but not aimed at the VC or NVA. They were convoys of ARVN trucks, all carrying large logs, probably mahogany, which grew in abundance in the region's forests. These were not destined to be part of defensive positions, mind you. This was private enterprise, ARVN style. The commanding officer and his subordinates had no doubt established a lucrative trade in several products, with the eventual user not inquired about. Using both military labor and military vehicles made this even more profitable, if at considerable expense to the unit's combat readiness.

Corruption was a problem in every ARVN/GVN unit at every level. It was everywhere, but it was most obvious in III Corps, which encompassed the area around the capital of Saigon, itself an autonomous city. The fundamental problem was that, as III Corps surrounded the capitol, so did the ARVN divisions assigned to secure it. The GVN had learned from hard experience that putting a competent, ambitious general in charge of troops a short drive from the capital was not a good idea. Long before my first visit, the survivors of this game of musical chairs made sure that the generals commanding III Corps were either too incompetent for men to follow, too corrupt to even be interested, or preferably both. This policy had stabilized the government, at the cost of allowing the VC/NVA to get close to the capitol without anybody noticing (or saying) anything.

There were many examples of this, but the most famous was the division whose men we saw laboring to enrich their commanders, the ARVN 18th Division. When the division was first formed and stationed in Hau Nghia, it was designated the 10th Division. Its sustained level of incompetence, corruption, and poor morale soon made it the target of that favorite jibe of both the Vietnamese and the Americans: "Number Ten!" Every Vietnamese knew the slang phrase, along with its opposite ("Number One!"), so the hapless ARVN unit became known to one and all as "the Number Ten Division." The scorn was so universal that the unit was redesignated the 18th Division, and was referred to as such officially. Unofficially, nothing changed; as a military unit, it remained Number Ten.

On one of these day trips, I didn't drive at all. My father had by this time been transferred to Saigon. He invited us to go with him to a factory in Binh Duong Province that produced a type of the plaster cast elephants that were quite popular. We accepted, and on the appointed Saturday he picked us up in one of the ubiquitous black Ford sedans. He had a driver, of course, a Vietnamese woman, which was a good thing because he didn't know the way. It was a pleasant trip, the "factory" was pre-industrial revolution, in both size and techniques, and we bought a pair of elephants. I have a basic memory of the trip and we still have the elephants, but I should have paid more attention to the driver. Within a few years she would become my stepmother.

Short Flights on Dubious Airlines

We flew out of country twice during my year in Saigon. The first was a conventional stay in Bangkok, where we did the conventional things. The second lasted longer and involved more flying. We decided to visit Cambodia and Laos, which at that time meant Phnom Penh and Vientiane. We knew we couldn't get outside of either town, as, although both were the capital cities of their respective nations, both were also just about the only territory the governments that resided in those cities could be said to control. Nothing outside either was accessible by Western civilians not employed by some government. As tourist locations, both cities could most charitably be described as "unspoiled." This included the lack of any ability to deal with tourists, albeit for good reasons. We thus did everything on our own, ad-libbing everything except the flight arrangements themselves. We undertook the two-stop trip by flying from Saigon to Phnom Penh on Air Vietnam, from Phnom Penh to Vientiane on Air Cambodge (the Cambodian state airline), and from Vientiane to Saigon on Royal Air Lao. This was the trifecta of dubious airlines, for sure. The planes were DC-4s in every instance, which at least meant a metal staircase to walk down to the tarmac on, a real luxury in an aeronautical world of tail-draggers. The other consideration, however, was that both were the airlines of states that had demonstrated a manifest inability to function as such. The conventional wisdom was that the maintenance for both the Cambodian and Lao airlines was done in Viet Nam by Vietnamese mechanics, which was not exactly a selling point either. Still, there being no other alternative we booked our flights. Each turned out to be uneventful, for which we were quite grateful.

Hotels—and everything else—were another matter. We knew of a hotel in Vientiane, so we could at least give our driver at the airport a name. But the only hotel we knew of in Phnom Penh was pretty much the only hotel anyone knew of, and it was always full. Once out of the terminal in Phnom Penh, we engaged the driver of an ancient and decrepit vehicle of apparently French design for a ride into town and asked for his recommendation. He took us to a simple but clean establishment that had open rooms for unexpected guests. We stayed two nights and left with nothing but good feelings about the efforts of our hosts.

Touring Phnom Penh meant two activities: (1) walking around town while trying to follow a map printed in French that quickly revealed itself to be out of date and (2) riding in pedal cyclos wherever the drivers saw fit to take us. The old pedal cyclo was an endangered species in motorized Saigon, but Phnom Penh's streets were a remarkable contrast. They were close to deserted, and cyclos fit our needs perfectly. We rode and walked around, following more or less along the Mekong waterfront, and photographed many beautiful buildings whose names and functions we would never learn. My Vietnamese was useless, but Barbara's French sufficed to get our basic needs—i.e., food and drink—met whenever necessary. Given what I knew about its Vietnamese ex-residents, my feelings were somewhat ambivalent; but the Cambodians we met were uniformly charming and polite, once past their initial shock at seeing an American couple there, of all places.

We did our share of wandering through the small street-side shops, and in one found some things we decided to buy. They were called "temple rubbings," thick parchment-like paper that is pressed, when wet, onto bas-relief sculptures on Khmer temples. When they dry, they are removed, then the raised parts are painted gold and the background painted black. They were quite impressive, particularly the one we found in a tall urn. It was huge, about 6 feet by 3 feet. We bought two other, much smaller ones. Rolled up, they were easy to carry onto the plane. Once back in Saigon, we had them all framed and set behind glass, and the large one became a particularly impressive wall decoration.

I had had no goals whatsoever about what to see in Phnom Penh, but I actually wanted to see one specific thing in Vientiane. It was known to the Americans as "the vertical airstrip," another of those items of the conventional wisdom that everyone seemed to know about, if not the details. As background, you need to understand that, by common agreement, the Lao people were—and, presumably, still are—one of the finest, gentlest, and least warlike people on the face of the earth. Compared to the Royal Lao Army, ARVN fought like tigers. We and the Communists had spent considerable time struggling against this characteristic in order to achieve our opposing goals, and the Communists had had much greater success. The American side, while ostensibly that of the generally recognized government (and even that was disputed), got its fighting done through the Montagnard peoples of Laos, primarily the Hmong. We just couldn't get the Lao to actually fight for us.

The CW was that, at some unremembered point, some U.S. advisors decided that an airstrip needed to be built somewhere and got the money appropriated for its construction. The Lao, however, instead used the money to construct a religious monument, an arch, in Vientiane itself. I'm sure it had a formal name, but I never learned it. We had no problem finding it. We hailed two cyclos, I simply said "vertical airstrip" in English to my cyclo driver, and he led us right to it. There it was, in Vientiane, and given its surroundings it was rather impressive. I have the photos to prove that it existed but nothing to back up the story of its origin; it was just part of the conventional wisdom at the time.

There was little else to see in Vientiane, which as a national capital would make a nice American county seat deep in the countryside. There was a bar "downtown" that magazine articles had identified as the center of the wild nightlife of the Americans stationed there. That may have been the case, but it was a little hole in the wall. We didn't go there either evening we were in Vientiane, and during the day it was closed.

The "Easter Offensive"

As the month of March 1972 ended, so did the good life of golf, parties, and day trips interspersed with some work. On March 30 NVA troops launched a massive attack across the DMZ, quickly overrunning the ARVN units stationed in the area. The NVA then attacked in II Corps at Kontum and later in III Corps. What became known as "the Easter Offensive" saw 12 NVA divisions, plus other individual units—over 200,000 men in all, including over 1,000 tanks—undertake a formal invasion. This was the greatest crisis to strike South Viet Nam since the Tet Offensive of '68. Considered as military operations, the two could not have been more different, but the Easter Offensive would pose a greater threat to the regime's existence than even Tet had. During the weekend, I listened to such news of the onslaught as I could (little real news made the initial broadcasts) and concluded the worst. The first thing Monday morning I called the staff together. "From this moment on," I told them, "we are going to be very busy." And so we came to be.

The ARVN, and therefore the GVN, teetered on the edge. The U.S. had only one real option, air power, and quickly applied it—in unprecedented amounts. U.S. Air Force units around the globe quickly found themselves involved. B-52s dropped some sixty million pounds of bombs around Kontum alone in 25 days during April and May 1972, and it was a secondary front.[4] The crisis on the ground even provoked the use of "Arc Light" formations (three B-52s in close formation releasing simultaneously at a carefully calculated point—absolutely devastating) as close ground support, which had previously been considered too dangerous to the nearby friendlies. The NVA persisted through this hell and came close to breaking the ARVN, but U.S. air power was the difference. The ARVN stiffened, then held, sheltering behind the rain of U.S. bombs.

The attacks generated what became a flood of refugees, particularly in I Corps, fleeing combat yet again. I, in turn, wondered—yet again—about the refugees in the camp at Cam Lo that I had visited in 1967 that was so close to the DMZ. If they had not had to flee at some earlier date they certainly had to flee this onslaught. The first calls from WVD in I Corps came in that Monday morning, crying for help, anything we could send. II Corps joined in, and the WVD Refugee Division shifted into crisis mode, attempting to collect the badly needed items and then get them to where they were needed, by far the greater problem. I Corps was farther away, but air transport of commodities within II Corps was insufficient to meet the general need, let alone a crisis like this one. The alternative, the few roads in the region, was worse, as each was subject to enemy attack at several points. Early on we even had to ask ourselves if we dared send anything to Da Nang, which itself might be overrun. We did whatever we could, because caution was irrelevant; if Da Nang fell, then the rest of the country would also. We sent everything we could and had to trust our I Corps WVD staff to distribute the most needed items to the most needy people. The Easter Offensive rapidly grew into an existential crisis for the RVN and, as it turned out, for the War Victims Directorate also.

In the middle of the first week the staff of the Refugee Division was summoned to a meeting and introduced to a U.S. Army major I will refer to as "Major Balls." He announced to us that he had been appointed to establish something called the "Refugee Operations Center." It would be an office, with him and a secretary. From now on, all communications from the provinces about their refugee situation and supply needs would go directly to him, not the WVD. He would then decide where the communication should go and direct the necessary response. This would, he claimed, make the response mechanism more efficient, as everything would be flowing thorough one spot (his office) and could quickly be assigned for action. He would then monitor our response and see that everything happened quickly and efficiently. He was very upbeat in the military manner about how his plan was needed for us to deal with the job that confronted us. We never learned whether Major Balls had this plan in his mind, just waiting for the time to propose it, or had simply seen an opportunity and quickly seized it. Whichever it was, he told us that he had already pitched this plan to higher-ups in CORDS and had received permission to go ahead, all without ever informing the people most involved, the WVD Refugee Division.

We of the Refugee Division staff sat and listened to this plan in stunned disbelief. A crisis had sent thousands of people fleeing and would generate thousands more in the next few days. Carrying what little they could of their possessions, these people desperately needed shelter, food, water, and virtually everything else people in peacetime take for granted. Their situation was desperate, and their government was hanging on by a thread. In the face of all this, the American response was a bureaucratic power play. Fortunately for those around me, I was so astonished it took a while before I got angry, and I got out of that meeting without exploding. But I did shortly thereafter, and poor Roy had to listen to me vent. The staff gathered together once we were back in our offices and gradually calmed down. How to deal with this? We simply didn't believe that adding a brand new level to the bureaucracy—for that's what Major Balls was going to do—could in any way improve our performance.

We ultimately decided to deal with the challenge by ignoring it. Our job was to get relief supplies to where the refugees were congregating, and that's what we continued to do. Our representatives at the regional and provincial level cooperated. We and they just continued to do our jobs, talking directly to one another (it was possible, if just, to have a telephone conversation in South Viet Nam) and arranging for shipments to be made. As far as we were concerned, Major Balls and his Refugee Operations Center did not exist. We copied him on some communications but made it clear he was in no way involved in the actual work. We knew we had Norm Hearns's bureaucratically knowledgeable help in this effort and appreciated it. He basically shielded us from whatever protests came to him from above. At some point in the following two months Major Balls disappeared. We didn't notice at the time and couldn't have cared less if we had noticed.

Some people have since termed this attack a "dress rehearsal" for April of 1975. They are wrong. The NVA meant to win, not practice, and they damn near did. It was a very near thing. Exactly three years later when I watched on American TV the final collapse and saw the chaos that the lack of contingency planning can cause, I wondered how much worse things would have been had the NVA attack in 1972 succeeded. The number of desperate Americans would have been much larger, with Barbara and I among them carrying what few belongings we could and leaving the rest behind. We would have been refugees, experiencing a properly ironic end to our experience.

Surplus Food

The early months of the Easter Offensive brought work enough for us all, but right in the middle of this a new opportunity presented itself. Or at least it seemed that way at first. We were even more in need of useful foodstuffs (not "Food for Peace") for the huge number of refugees that continued to be generated when an opportunity to obtain some seemed to just drop out of the sky. This was in the form of computer printouts, the old page-connected type, and they dropped out of Roy Fontall's hands and onto my desk. "I know you're busy," he said, "but this could be an opportunity to get the food we need." I began to investigate this new development.

What I was scanning was evidence that the drawdown of Americans in Viet Nam had reached major proportions. I have always suspected that somehow, somewhere, someone had calculated what an American soldier needs, from rifles to toothpaste. Multiply each of those amounts by the number of personnel in country, and you have the amount of each item you need to sustain our entire effort, wherever we are. I was scanning the food portion of the total list, and it was huge. At this point, almost all the U.S. combat and support troops had been withdrawn. Thus we had in country a great deal of material now considered "surplus," because it existed in greater amounts than the current personnel number called for.

As Americans continued to leave, that surplus would only continue to grow. So, how to get rid of those things we didn't want to ship back? Everyone had heard the whispered CW stories about vehicles buried, entrepreneurial supply officers (and sergeants) making some side money, and the like. Well, when it came to food, the answer was to list the items and amounts available and offer to distribute them. First come, first served.

The lists were huge, as the items were unbelievable in both variety and amount. They were not prepared food but all the components needed to do the preparation, American style. I remember quickly losing track of how much gelatin—not the flavored kind, just the basic, flavorless item—was available, just one of the enormous number of offerings. The basic problem, of course, was that the food items on the list were to prepare the American diet, not the Vietnamese. I did find some entries for rice, flour, salt, and some other useful items. I carefully checked off the items WVD would like delivered to our warehouses in Tu Duc and returned the request form. It took a few days for a response, and it didn't come the way I had expected it. I got a phone call from the U.S. advisor at the warehouse, who asked me, "Where do you expect me to put the 72 tractor-trailer loads of food that are coming?" All I managed to say in reply was, "What?" The first tractor-trailers had just arrived, carrying the notice of how many more were coming. I dropped everything and immediately drove out to Tu Duc. Only a few more trucks had arrived by the time I arrived, and the advisor had, on his own, put a hold on any further shipments. After expressing my sincere gratitude, I examined the manifests that told us of what had come and what was coming. It was clear that no one had even looked at our checked items. We had become a destination, nothing more. "They" apparently decided just what and how much to ship. We didn't receive any of the items we had requested, just large amounts of useless foodstuffs, useless, that is, for Vietnamese. And yes, one of those loads was all gelatin. We never learned why they decided to send 72 trailer loads, but at least we stopped that early. I now had entirely too much of the WVD warehouse capacity filled with utterly useless items and no idea of what to do with them.

An opportunity arose within a few days, and it could not have come from a more unexpected source. I was sitting at my desk when a Vietnamese secretary approached me and said, "Lieutenant Colonel Ba is here to see you." I could not have been more surprised. Lt. Col. Ba NEVER, repeat NEVER, so much as acknowledged an American advisor, let alone came to USAID II to see one. It had never happened, yet here he was asking for me and not Roy. Roy was elsewhere at the time, so I utilized his office to receive Lt. Col. Ba, as my desk was merely one of several in a large room (I told you "Deputy Chief of the Refugee Division" was no big thing). I had begun to recover from the shock, and even to suspect why Lt. Col. Ba might be here to see me, when our secretary ushered him into Roy's office, with me at Roy's desk. Lt, Col. Ba actually spoke English to me and had brought no interpreter. He came right to the point, and smiling his broadest he pointed out that we needed to get the U.S. military's surplus food "to the refugees." He had good sources of information, that was for sure. He even knew that Roy had delegated me to be in charge of the program and didn't even bother with the formality of going through him. That meant somebody inside our office was a spy for the MSW, yet another of so many little, unsolved mysteries. What followed was a conversation wherein I told him, both politely and quite indirectly, that we at WVD might be using a small portion of the program, but that it would be handled through our warehouses and under our control. He persisted, but by now I knew how to politely deflect a conversation, having been instructed previously by several versions of Lt. Col. Ba. He left smiling but unhappy, I had no doubt. I never saw him again.

It was only later that evening, as I sat thinking about this strange day, that it occurred to me that I had probably just passed up an opportunity to make some money on the side, maybe a lot. With Lt. Col. Ba's reputation, a few properly chosen words about my importance to his getting any foodstuffs might have been quite productive. I could have been "The Surplus Food King of Viet Nam!" Oh, well.

That Last Trip

I did get away from the constant deluge at the office one other time, although again not by choice. I walked into the office early one morning only to be collared by Roy and told of a change in plans. He was scheduled to go on another flight with Dr. Dan, but for some reason (he didn't explain and I didn't ask) he couldn't go. I had to take his place and leave immediately for the Air America terminal at the airport. I was not pleased, as there was much to do in the office, but I held my tongue. I thought the trip was going to be another dog and pony show, of no significance. I was wrong—very, very wrong. That day turned out to be the most memorable one I ever spent in Viet Nam. It had no discernable theme, instead offering, one after another, so many of the absurdities that characterized this conflict.

Dr. Dan, three members of his staff, and I climbed into a Pilatus Porter and departed. I had neglected to ask where we were going, and my attention was so soon diverted that I never learned. We flew southwest, and to my surprise we were soon flying over water, nothing but water. This was the first time I had seen the Mekong River in full flood, and I was unprepared for the fact that the *entire province* to which we were flying was underwater. The water was only a few feet deep but so laden with silt that the ground below it was invisible. It was as if we were flying over some vast lake, perfectly still, with only a few tree lines and clusters of small buildings on stilts visible. Then we landed on a short asphalt airstrip immediately adjoining some buildings, all located on a rectangular-shaped island built up amid all that water. It came up all of a sudden, as we were at low altitude, and the little Porter set us down quickly. I looked around me and saw nothing but water around this little artificial island. As a veteran of the Central Highlands, my disorientation was complete. We deplaned, and I immediately retreated to the rear fringes of the group and let Dr. Dan receive his due from the assembled GVN officials who were there to greet him. We all were loaded into jeeps and Scouts and driven a very short distance to what must have been province headquarters. There followed a short (and hushed, as I could not hear what was being said) conference. I went to the rear of the room and found a U.S. advisor to tell me what was going on.

He said that this visit was, indeed, a morale-boosting event, and the province greatly needed such a boost. The province headquarters had been overrun about a month earlier and the Province Chief killed. This should have been big news, and I was surprised that I had not heard of it. An event of that nature should have been in *Stars and Stripes* or we should have heard of it through channels if war victims had been generated, but those in Saigon knew nothing. It turned out there was a good reason for this. Had the province HQ been overrun by the enemy it would have been embarrassing enough, but the enemy had nothing to do with it. The province HQ had been overrun by the ARVN unit assigned to protect it. It seems that the Province Chief and ARVN commander had been engaged in an evening of drinking and gambling, which climaxed in a disagreement that got out of control. The province chief summoned a few aides and had the ARVN commander thrown out bodily from the compound. The ARVN commander then returned to his unit, roused some of his men, armed them, and attacked the provincial headquarters. They met little resistance and soon captured the Province Chief, whom the ARVN commander promptly shot. I would never hear or read anything about this event in the press.

I had no idea what, if anything, was accomplished at that secretive, hushed conference, but when Dr. Dan and his entourage began to depart, I joined them. This conference also seemed to have concluded whatever real business Dr. Dan was there to conduct, as from that point on we were basically tourists being shown around. We all went outside and I saw that a VNAF chopper had been started and was awaiting us. This gave me pause. I had never flown on a VNAF plane before, let alone a helicopter. Americans held VNAF helicopter pilots in contempt, for their refusal to do what they had been trained to do (and often charging money to evacuate specific wounded, for example), but my concern had nothing to do with that. My fear was the awareness, common to every American, of the Vietnamese antipathy to performing preventative maintenance. No one else showed any trepidation, however (I was the only American in the party), so we boarded, the pilots pulled pitch, and we took off.

A short flight brought us to a joint RF/PF and American District Team compound, all on small, elevated piles of land considerably smaller than at the province headquarters. Before approaching, the Huey flew over and around a village of two dirt streets, intersecting in the form of a cross. The community appeared to be prosperous. Each foot of land frontage along the water's edge was taken up by buildings, from small, ramshackle residences to more substantial structures, although all were largely open, of course, due to the climate. The front of each building lay on one of the two intersecting strips of land. The remainder of each was located on pilings over the water that surrounded each arm of the cross. This was even true of by far the largest structure, a Catholic church, located at one corner of the intersecting streets. It appeared that every resident lived within this compact array, at least during the flood season.

Our landing spot was a floating dock, which at that time had some issue, as one of its corners was underwater, giving it an insubstantial look for a place to set down. The VNAF pilot put the craft down expertly, however. No one ever complained about a VNAF chopper pilot's lack of skill.

We were greeted by a captain, a member of the district advisory team who apologized to us for the DSA not being present, saying he was with a visiting general on "the dredge." I didn't have time to inquire what "the dredge" was, but was ushered into one of two open metal boats, each powered by an outboard motor. They were the advisory team's transportation during the flood season. We were taken to the cross-shaped town we had just flown over, stepped off the boats, and walked directly to the Catholic church.

It was lunchtime, and a meal was waiting for us. We were ushered into a sizeable room that had tables set in rows. The village's Catholic priest greeted us and motioned for us to take seats. We did and I found myself about in the middle row, surrounded by Vietnamese but next to the American captain who had greeted us. Lunch was delicious, built around fish and shellfish caught just outside the door, the captain told me. Then I noticed that an American, also a priest, had joined the company and was sitting next to the village priest. When I asked about him, the captain described him as "the priest's pet American." He had apparently shown up (before the captain, who was just passing along what he knew, had arrived) in country on his own and was not affiliated with any of the Catholic relief organizations that had a substantial presence. God had called him, and he answered. He somehow managed to meet the priest who was our host and had been taken to live with him. The captain explained that the American priest was very useful begging needed things or services from American military units. No one wanted to say no to a priest, particularly an American one.

I was seated close enough to realize that the two priests would occasionally speak to each other, but just far enough away to make the words indistinct and unclear. I could tell that they weren't speaking English, Vietnamese, or French, and I was intrigued. Puzzled, I turned again to the captain, who replied, "Our priest speaks Vietnamese, Chinese, and French, but no English; the American speaks only English. So they talk to each other in Latin." With that, I remembered my high school Latin teacher, who had so passionately and so often proclaimed, "Latin is not a dead language!" He would have been overjoyed to learn that in this obscure corner of Southeast Asia, Latin was still a living language. After the extended lunch, the captain directed me back to the advisory team's boat and we set out again, following the boat carrying Dr. Dan and his staff. I, who did not know where I was, was now heading off to somewhere else, in this enormous, horizon-filling body of water with neither wave nor current.

Somewhere else turned out to be yet another strange sight in this bizarre world of water, a large dredge. This contraption was sitting surrounded by water and patiently working its way back and forth across a small portion of that water, being alternately pulled by one or the other of two cables that extended in front and to each side. The slurry the dredge produced came out a chute and was being deposited in piles on each side of whatever it was the dredge was digging. This was yet another incongruous sight on a day already brimming with them. I expected to see a dredge working along a discernable channel, with land not far away, but this one was working away in the middle of a liquid vastness, and I had no idea what it was doing. We made fast to the dredge, climbed aboard, and proceeded to the top deck. There we were served light refreshments and drinks, joining the Vietnamese District Chief, an American brigadier general who, remarkably enough, had only one aide with him, and an American major, the DSA. We did introductions all around, but by this time my brain was going into a sensory overload of strangeness and I forgot everyone's name right away. I regretted that later, particularly regarding the general. He delivered the crowning moment of absurdity on this day spent viewing several contenders for the title, and he deserves to be remembered.

We recent arrivals joined the party already underway, with pleasantries all around. Dr. Dan waxed eloquent about South Viet Nam's economic potential, particularly the Mekong Delta. As it turned out, the dredge, "the largest dredge in Southeast Asia," he claimed, was widening and deepening an existing canal that was invisible during this flood time but was no doubt important when the water receded. I took their word for it about what the dredge was doing; I saw only the fact that it was also creating small portions of land that, being above the flood level, would certainly become valuable, and I wondered who was going to get them.

The general joined our party in the DSA's boat as we again departed, following the District Chief in his boat and Dr. Dan and his staff in another, bound for where I once again had no idea. The journey took a little while and gave me a few opportunities to observe yet again the GVN's attitude toward those on whose support it depended. We passed a few sampans, those small, oared, low-freeboard vessels that were so evident in Viet Nam wherever there was water. Each carried one or two people. The District

Chief and his staff, in the two leading boats, would never slow when passing a sampan; they just roared by, the boat's wake coming close to sinking those low little boats and leaving each lurching alarmingly as they sped away. The American DSA and our boat, by contrast, would always slow to "no wake" speed until we were past the sampan, then accelerate again to catch up. I had by that time seen far too many examples of the GVN's imperious attitude toward its own population for such things to be remarkable, but this near swamping of sampans was one of the most memorable examples, if only because it was so casual.

When the District Chief's boat began to slow down we knew we were nearing our destination. This turned out to be three flat, artificially circular islands, each about 50 feet in diameter, laid out so that they constituted the corners of a triangle. Flimsy bamboo bridges connected the three islands. Two of them held one artillery piece each behind a curved revetment of wooden boxes. The third island, slightly farther away from the other two, held the living quarters of the military unit stationed there. The quarters were roofed over and personal gear was strewn about. The occupants stared out at us.

None of this made much sense to me. This little firebase did have some sections of B-40 wire strung between poles that covered a small part of what was a 360-degree perimeter, and anyone attacking the base would have to do so in boats. But it still didn't look very defensible, at least to this civilian. The curved revetment of wooden boxes behind which each gun nestled was not much protection, as the boxes obviously contained the shells for the guns to fire—not something you would want to crouch behind if people were shooting at you. This is where the American general stepped in and explained what I was seeing. This was one of several such bases, he explained, each part of an intricate defense system. No firebase could be defended solely by its occupants, by design. Each base had the exact coordinates of every base within range of its guns and radio communications with those bases, so that artillery fire from the others could be called in if necessary and delivered on target immediately. This was an interlocking system, insuring mutual security over a broad area.

And then the general said, "At least that's the theory." At that my ears perked up. He continued, saying that while this was a tried and true defense system, the local geography required that the guns be replaced with the change of seasons. During the dry season the islands would support 155mm howitzers, while during the flood season they would support only 105mm ones. These were exchanged in the only possible way, by helicopter, twice a year. And so it had been, but now the Americans were gone, leaving VNAF to make the exchanges. This was the flood season, and these were 105mm howitzers, he said, pointing to both guns. "But now look closely at those wooden boxes," he said. I did, and after some searching I found what he was directing me toward. Unbelieving, I looked at another one and then several others. Each box in that curved revetment was stenciled "155mm." The guns had been exchanged but not the ammunition. These guns could not shoot. None of the Vietnamese said that, of course, during the visit, nor would they. They all carried on as if this was a conventional morale-building visit. The soldiers stationed here certainly needed some morale building, living as they were in total isolation, aware that they could not do their job and that all the boring time spent here was pointless. The oversight of the ammunition also meant that any other isolated location that depended on supporting fire from this base was out of luck. And sitting in their own indefensible location, could they depend on support fire from any other base—or had that little oversight about the ammunition been typical and not confined to their little location?

This was total farce, but everyone played their part with a straight face. The District Chief maintained his air of command to impress the visiting dignitaries; Dr. Dan just shook hands, not inquiring into the obvious; and the soldiers themselves sat silently, watching it all. The American general could, of course, have interrupted this little charade, but he revealed the truth only to me, I guess because I was the only person in the party that did not realize what was actually going on. Somewhat later I began to see this last little vignette as symbolic of the entire American involvement in Viet Nam. The carefully designed mutual defense system the U.S. had installed in that area had been rendered useless by overlooking merely one component among the many that needed to be managed. And so it was in Viet Nam itself. We showed up in an isolated little place that was not much touched by Western influence outside the few cities. To save it from Communism we designed, built, and implemented a complex, multilayered military structure. To us this was merely standard operating procedure, if rather larger than any previously attempted. The multilayered complexity required an interdependency that was also standard for us— but not for our targeted users. The structure functioned only when given constant maintenance and extensive lubrication, i.e., gasoline and oil, but mainly personal attention. We could operate this structure and we could do our level best to train our clients how to do the same, but even in the face of overwhelming evidence that they couldn't we kept to the program. When we left, necessary actions began to be left undone, and the very structure we had taught ARVN to depend on began to unravel. In such a top-down authority structure, few had the guts to point out that it was all a pointless farce.

On the flight home, I kept telling myself, *Memorize what happened today, go over it again and again, don't forget!* Another part of me was saying, *No one back in "the world" will ever believe you!*

Short

The surreal journey to the Mekong Delta was the last trip I took during my time in Saigon. We had plenty of work to do and I kept at it to the end of my tour, in early July 1972. By that point, the U.S. effort in Viet Nam was in the final stages of drawdown. The combat military had virtually all left, and MACV was shrinking also. The civilian members of CORDS were the easiest targets. We were temporary employees, hired for the duration, and that duration was up once our current tour was. Virtually everyone with a /L after their rank was being RIFed. We weren't being terminated in the middle of a tour (which accounted for the continuous shuffle of people into slots), but everyone who applied for another tour would be told no, and, as we were "limited" to work in Viet Nam, that would be that. The steadily diminishing number of slots in each directorate would be occupied by the regular Rs, on a decidedly temporary basis, as even their slots would be eliminated eventually.

Given the nature of the USAID bureaucracy, everyone believed that there would be exceptions to this policy because there were exceptions to every policy. Others may have heard of exceptions, but I was actually offered one. My father (who was one of those who successfully removed their /Ls and went on to a long second career with USAID) informed me (entirely unofficially, of course) that "Bill" Colby had told him that if I applied for a second tour, I would be accepted. This would be the first step to getting the /L removed from my title. Thus, most unexpectedly, an opportunity to do something close to what I had wanted to do since early adolescence appeared before me. But by then it was too late. I was not going to accept Ambassador Colby's intervention for another tour because I was not going to apply for one. I had decided to leave, regardless. I could no longer evade or dodge that increasingly repeated question in my mind: WHAT AM I DOING HERE? On one level, what was I actually accomplishing? Evidence of that was impossible to find; the light at the end of the tunnel was no closer than before. So, on a deeper level, what was I doing here? That is to say, did I want to continue to do it? The answer was no. This was a momentous decision, easily the most significant one up to that point, and, upon decades of reflection, perhaps of my whole life.

I had enjoyed my time in Lam Dong Province, at least while I had had something meaningful to do. I had gotten along well with the Vietnamese and was, by American standards, tolerant of their shortcomings, the majority of which were our fault anyway. Not so with my fellow Americans. I simply held them—and myself—to a much higher standard. Far too often in far too many ways we (and I definitely include myself) had fallen short. After all, we were the ones over there, telling them what to do, killing those who didn't agree, ruining their countryside (not to mention their morals), and all the while expecting them to be grateful. They weren't, in the slightest. In the final analysis, of course, the payment for our folly would be extracted from those we left behind, not us.

Once I got to Saigon and began to work primarily with other Americans, things began to go downhill. I had long since ceased to support the war, even before I accepted a job with USAID. I had been able to rationalize my core dilemma with the fact that I was there to help people, not just improve the workings of the GVN. As my time in country increased, this became increasingly harder to do. I had no tolerance at all for the almost universal deception practiced by CORDS, that ever-so-casual and step-by-step alteration of reports to demonstrate that we were actually "winning" the war. I, on more than one occasion, had succumbed to the temptation to tell the honest truth as I saw it, despite the ample evidence that to do so would be pointless. I just couldn't help it. As the end of my second year in country approached, I began to understand that this characteristic would not be helpful in future USAID contexts. My time with CORDS had demonstrated that trying to fit into a structure where the point was to avoid offending anyone by saying anything close to the truth had proved much too difficult. A career with USAID seemed to offer a lifetime of this. Such a career would compensate by enveloping me in that luxurious cocoon that surrounds the American government civilian overseas, where the pain stemming from the lack of any real achievement on the job was made tolerable by the combination of a living standard far above that you could have back in the USA and the dulling effects of alcohol.

In the final analysis, I had to own up to the by now indisputable fact that of the all the words that have been used to describe me, "diplomatic" ranks low on the list. I, who had desired to join the diplomatic corps since adolescence, had to confront the truth: I was simply not suited for that kind of work. I informed my father of my decision. He was not pleased but accepted my decision with good grace. He had envisioned us seeing each other again in the far regions of the globe, but it was not to be.

WVD Deputy Director Hearns presenting me with a plaque at my departure ceremony, July 1972.

A Spear-Carrier in Viet Nam

In early July 1972 I had to formally process out at USAID I and supervise the packers of our apartment furniture (and my Suzuki bike), then turn over the keys. We hadn't accumulated much in the way of furniture but had purchased some souvenirs. Most were from Viet Nam, but some were from both Cambodia and Thailand, including the large temple rubbing. All of this—and the two cats we had by then—were packed up and shipped home to Pennsylvania.[5] I don't remember if I gifted the jeep to anyone in particular. My departure was decidedly anticlimactic because departures were the order of business in CORDS at that time. We had a round of parties with friends, primarily Barbara's work colleagues at Land Reform, then concluded with a ceremony before the Refugee Division staff, where Deputy Director Hearns gave me a plaque commemorating my service and a GVN civilian medal. And then we left, to take the slow way home—via Hong Kong, Singapore, and Bali—to Pennsylvania, where we would await word that our Winnebago was ready. After that we would spend a winter in Mexico.

I was returning to "The World," but it would be a different world. Jim, Jimi, and Janis were dead, and I had no Plan B. My future was totally uncertain, but I did know one thing: I wanted to do something that when I went home at night would exist when it hadn't before and be something good. I had never felt that way in Viet Nam.

Epilogue

"Their Vietnamese fight harder than our Vietnamese"

This phrase expressed a truth so self-evident that we CORDS officers didn't bother uttering it; we just spoke of the latest examples. Those of us at my level observed it among everything the GVN organized for defense, including the RD Cadre and the Regional/Popular Force units. Some of our military members had served previous tours as MACV advisors to ARVN units, and they told the same stories about those ARVN units that were supposedly the basis for GVN security. We civilians listened and acted accordingly. That was just the way things were. If you assumed this and acted appropriately you were a lot less likely to be unpleasantly surprised or even dead. It wasn't a subject you thought about in any detail because that would have called into question virtually everything else. We each had a job to do, and we did it, also doing our best to avoid the broader questions.

I left Viet Nam in July 1972 convinced that it was only a matter of time before "our side" collapsed, so the events of spring 1975 were not really a surprise. Still, the horrible nature of the collapse, particularly that in the Central Highlands, the part of the country that had become dear to me, shocked me profoundly. The retreat was not planned; the ARVN army commanders and province chiefs simply fled, followed by those of enough rank to grab a plane or helicopter. Order and discipline collapsed and were replaced with blind panic. The troops, now leaderless, were ordered to retreat down a minor road totally unsuited to the traffic that was to use it. The result was not just chaos; it was savagery, the strong—like those driving tanks—bullying their way to the front, leaving a disorganized mob that began to feed on itself. During those tragic weeks in

Epilogue

1975 no component of South Viet Nam's military or civilian leadership delivered the service that so many had tried so hard to inculcate in them, but those in the Central Highlands performed the worst.

The shameful manner in which our grand experiment in "nation building" had come to an end also reawakened questions I had long sought to suppress. They all revolved around the question of "Why should this have been?" Some years later, when the opportunity presented itself, I began graduate studies in history. Viet Nam was the dominant topic in my studies. I read almost every book available on the subject (there were many), I used Vietnamese to meet the foreign language requirement for a PhD, and I even delivered a paper on development efforts in Viet Nam to the Society for Historians of American Foreign Relations (SHAFR) at an annual conference. The opinions expressed below are thus the result of my amalgamation of personal experience and academic study.

Regardless of one's political inclinations, personal connections to the war, or any other of the many possible influencers of opinion, there are some basic facts that cannot be ignored. We spent nearly two decades of active involvement in a war to preserve an independent South Viet Nam and we failed miserably. During our second decade we did all that American destructive technology could do to convince the leaders of the North to abandon their attempt to complete what had been denied them in 1954. We bombed and strafed them, dropped deadly chemicals on them, and, in so doing, killed uncounted thousands of them. The physical destruction was staggering. And we kept it up, as only we can, year after year.

Yet they kept coming. They came despite ample knowledge that we owned the air, both day and night. At any moment they could be obliterated by an "Arc Light" strike, before anyone on the ground could even realize what was happening. Or it could have been napalm, dropped more visibly from a much smaller airplane, that would envelop them in one final, horrendously painful moment on this earth. Or it could just come slowly, from disease or some minor injury, because medical facilities were usually nonexistent. But still they kept coming, despite death being dealt them in many other, equally lethal, ways. And once they got there, they knew they would have the advantage of surprise, but that the U.S. would quickly respond with tactical air support for those they had caught unprepared. If they stood and fought, they were going to die. Most melted away before this could happen, but when ordered to do so they stood, they fought savagely, and they died. Yes, some were found with "born in the

180

North to die in the South" tattooed on their arms, and a few may even have had to be chained to the seats of their tanks, as reports claim. This is perfectly understandable, given the inevitability of their service and the huge odds against their survival.

What is less understandable is why the Vietnamese on "our" side—those who were not bombed or strafed whenever they showed their heads during daylight, or tracked down at night by sensors, who had air support, medical evacuation capability, and actual hospitals not too far away—so lacked the basic soldierly qualities that their adversaries demonstrated on a continuous basis. I think it safe to say that the average soldier in the NVA was not any happier about his life than his ARVN counterpart. Physically, he was much worse off in virtually every way. But he fought harder than his southern opponents, demonstrating a dedication and resolve that Americans could only dream that "our" Vietnamese would ever demonstrate. Patriotism, commitment, and bravery were the rule in the VC and the NVA; they were the exception in the ARVN, the Rfs and PFs, and on down the line.

We Americans take it for granted that service in the military instills patriotism; we see evidence of that truth all around us. We were not able to instill that fundamental component of any true army into the ARVN or even those forces designed for local self defense, despite trying hard and spending a great deal of money on the effort. Most of us civilians working in the pacification effort thought we knew the cause: corruption. We usually heard of military incompetence second hand, but we each personally experienced civilian corruption. Corruption's manifest existence was visible everywhere at every level in the GVN/ARVN. It was the lubricant of daily life, sloshing around everywhere. Everyone, civilian as well as military, saw a connection between pervasive corruption and military incompetence. We saw the former as a cause, the latter as a result, but this form of corruption took place far outside and above our area of responsibility, so we soldiered on with what we had to do. But we were wrong; corruption and incompetence were both results, and of the same cause.

What was that cause? What did the VC and NVA possess that our side lacked? The answer is actually quite simple. Call it *"something to fight for."* The other side had it, in spades. Ours didn't. Ho Chi Minh, Vo Nguyen Giap, and the others became mythic figures, but each had a core of patriotism and high ability. Ho was a Communist to us, but to everyone else he was a symbol of national resistance against the foreigner—the French then the Americans. That was a cause to fight—and die—for, and those willing to do so, and to suffer almost unimaginable horror in the process, could be counted in the millions.

The peoples on our side fought with us for a great variety of reasons, but precious few of them fought for a national identity. A cause and its symbols must have a broad attraction, and the Republic of Viet Nam was attractive mainly to those who could milk it for profit. It had no cause and no symbols because it had no substance, no reason for being. The Government of the Republic of Viet Nam rotted from the top down. In the final analysis, the Viet Nam war was not about defeating the enemy on the battlefield. *That* we did. We won the "conventional" war by any reckoning; we never lost a major battle and never lost any ground we didn't later retake. We inflicted huge casualties on our enemies and devastated their rear areas. Yet "The Other War" was the one that truly counted, and we lost it. In the final analysis, the fundamental U.S. task was to create a nation out of the stub of a land with only part of the people. We created a military in our own image to protect this new country and forced on its government several Western concepts of governmental responsibility, in order to, in that hackneyed phrase, "win the hearts and minds of the people." With that accomplished, we reasoned, the Vietnamese people would gratefully and courageously defend this new state. The evidence that we failed in this task is final and conclusive.

There were numerous reasons why we failed, but the unfortunate truth is that the seeds of collapse and disgrace were already planted when we arrived. We nurtured them, oversaw their growth as their intertwined vines took the country totally under their sway, and tried mightily to teach them how to do their real job. They were the senior military leadership of the Vietnamese armed forces. Describing the highest level of the GVN/ARVN officer corps, Ronald H. Spector, in *After Tet: The Bloodiest Year in Vietnam*, describes this group better than I ever could: "None of these men, indeed almost no member of the officer corps, had joined the great struggle for national independence from 1946 to 1954. Instead they had been the supporters and collaborators of the French, just as they now appeared to many Vietnamese to be the tools and proxies of the Americans. It was a group whose behavior was shaped by the firm conviction that no duty or obligation of citizenship was so compelling that it could not be avoided through judicious use of money and family connections, nor any position of trust so exalted that it could not be obtained by those same means."[1] We bet that the few who had joined the French during that war would provide the necessary leadership and inspiration for our war, despite virtually all the evidence being to the contrary. We foisted on the southern half of a people a regime of individuals that combined both incompetence and corruption to a degree rarely seen, even in our checkered career of supporting tin-pot military dictators. We backed them anyway and continued to do so, despite ample evidence that they had no desire to fight their countrymen and were instead engaged in enriching themselves through our largess. And we just kept doing it, because once you have committed "national prestige" to a project, abandoning that project becomes unthinkable.

True to this axiom, we just kept pushing chips on the table, and too many of those were of flesh and blood because they had the least value of those participating in the game. We accepted the corrupt and incompetent French-trained leadership and then proceeded to extend the corruption down the social structure by overwhelming a small society with money and creating a pantheon of illicit ways to earn it. In the process, we flooded their land with irresistible foreignness. We Americans continuously deluded ourselves that we weren't replacing the French, we were just helping the Vietnamese. That distinction was utterly lost on the Vietnamese people, who saw their new leaders were actually their old leaders-in-training now learning a different Western language. In the final analysis "Armin the ARVN" and his like down the military structure had only two reasons to fight: for himself and for his family, and the two often intertwined. The result was corruption and military incompetence because both motives place a high premium on staying alive.

If your primary goal is staying alive, you will not be very good at activities that require you to risk your life. Wearing a uniform, carrying a gun, and shooting it at someone else is simply foolish behavior, as virtually every Vietnamese spear-carrier recruited into that vast organizational web that was the GVN/ARVN knew for sure. Every one of them also knew that those on the other side did not share in that primary goal and were prepared to punish anyone who dared challenge it. The result was decades of small preparations for the final, total humiliation of April 1975.

I believe I have made it clear that I was one of the more forgiving (or, perhaps, "understanding") people among the Americans on the subject of corruption. Let me now make it equally clear that I did not then, and do not now, blame that multitude of Vietnamese we CORDS field-level advisors dealt with for either their corruption or their military incompetence. The Vietnamese with whom I and the other Americans worked were spear-carriers, just as we were, but with a great deal more at stake. I was there as a volunteer; for them, it was a matter of life and death, with no other place to go. No one had asked for their opinion or even desired it. No one had given them much choice about which side to "choose" and what they would be required to do. They just did what they had to do, with the primary goal that of simply staying alive. They were given a great deal to fight with but nothing to fight for. Facing those in the exact opposite condition, the result was inevitable.

Those at the top who told the spear-carriers where to go and what to do got out and went on to live their lives in comfort. As ex-President Thieu walked toward the helicopter that would take him into exile he was followed by aides carrying bags that clinked as the group strode quickly to safety. Those bags were filled with gold bars. But the farther down the ladder you were the less secure your escape plans, unless you happened to be a helicopter pilot who could fly his family to safety or at least make one last financial killing charging for a ride.

It would have been bad enough had the debacle—and subsequent bloodlettings—been confined to Viet Nam, but it wasn't. Laos was included, as all knew it would be, and the Hmong people we had recruited, paid, and fed faced genocide. Not enough of them got out. But no one foresaw what was going to happen to Cambodia. This has been the result of the war in Viet Nam that has affected me the most. My brief encounter with the young men we were sending to die for nothing has coalesced into a lifetime memory, buttressed by subsequent headlines. After 1975 the Khmer Rouge killed—through murder, starvation, and illness—approximately 1.7 million Cambodians out of a population of about 7 million. Blame whom you will for Viet Nam, but Richard Nixon and Henry Kissinger bear the blame for this horror.

As I write these final words, Henry Kissinger is still alive. Even after all these years, I on occasion amuse myself with some thoughts about what should happen to him after he dies. He's going to Hell, of course, but he shouldn't get the conventional treatment. No hellfire and brimstone, being one of countless massed souls ceaselessly toiling under whips while their bodies are rent asunder, none of that. I devoutly hope that he spends eternity in the backseat of an automobile sitting next to Richard Nixon, who began the journey before him. It should be hot, but the enervating, oppressive heat of the Vietnamese lowlands, alternating between humid and dry. As they drive along, all they can see are two lines of men walking along both sides of the road. These men are young, with tousled black hair and happy smiles, wearing their new uniforms and carrying their new rifles, utterly unaware of what awaits them. The ride is endless, as are the lines of young men. Kissinger and Nixon know that each and every one of them will be dead within a few years, sacrificed in a hopeless and valueless little "sideshow" because of the tragic combination of ego and ignorance of these two men. I fervently pray that these doomed men are all both Henry Kissinger and Richard Nixon will ever see, for all eternity.

Chapter Notes

Chapter One

1. An acronym for Civil Operations Revolutionary Development Support, the joint military-civilian pacification effort, about which more in Chapter Three.

2. It was a vain hope. The citadel was the site of fierce fighting during Tet of '68. The NVA units there resisted to the end, and the area suffered greatly from both ground combat and U.S. bombing attacks. Fighting in 1972 and 1975 added to the destruction. I understand that little of the "Forbidden City" itself remains.

3. I, of course, forgot their names shortly after leaving. While writing this book, I contacted Wycliffe, and they put me in touch with Carolyn. I engaged in a rewarding e-mail correspondence with her and learned the basic facts. She confirmed that she delivered her third child at Da Nang in August 1967. Their two older children were with them when I visited, but I did not see them. Their family was evacuated just before the onset of the Tet of '68 offensive. They remained in Viet Nam, and she, John, and their youngest daughter were taken prisoner in April 1975. They were kept in makeshift prison camps for months before finally being sent to the infamous Son Tay POW camp just outside Hanoi. They were finally released, together with others captured with them, as the "Ban Me Thuot 14." Carolyn tells their story in *Captured!*, which is available on Kindle and highly recommended. You won't believe what they went through!

Chapter Two

1. This policy was part of the attempt to correct, at least to some degree, the endemic problem of the American advisory effort: the 1-year tour. As John Paul Vann put it in 1963, "We don't have 12 years experience in this country. We have one year's experience twelve times." Under the short-tour system, a new MACV advisor would barely learn about his location and the nature of his job before he left and was replaced by someone who had to go through the same experience for himself. The result was no institutional memory and greatly diminished effectiveness by the American advisors. The 18/24 policy improved the situation, but not much.

2. The sequence of the tones is how we were taught; my Vietnamese-English dictionary has them in a different order.

3. "Viet Nam," properly rendered, means "Pacified South." The irony is overwhelming.

Chapter Three

1. There were three such USAID buildings. USAID I was USAID proper

and USAID II was CORDS. I never visited USAID III.

Chapter Four

1. Everyone called them "refugees," but officially they were "people fleeing Communism" (*Dong Bao Ti Nang Cong San*), although the overwhelming majority were, in fact, fleeing American firepower.

Chapter Five

1. This was the only time I ever saw Cobras flown by VNAF. I have read more than one claim that none were supplied to VNAF, yet I did see two.

2. This work was performed by civilian contractors and was entirely separate from the construction projects of the army engineers and navy Seabees.

3. For some quirky reason, probably deriving from my previous work as a bartender, I clearly remember that a quart of Jack Daniels Black Label went for $2.44, and I didn't even drink the stuff.

4. Thomas P. McKenna, *Kontum*, 257.

5. The frame of the large temple rubbing was broken in transit, obviously on impact, but somehow the glass within was not—one final mystery.

Epilogue

1. Ronald H. Spector, *After Tet*, 100–101.

Bibliography

Books

Allen, George W. *None So Blind: A Personal Account of the Intelligence Failure in Vietnam.* Chicago: Ivan R. Dee, 2001.

Herring, George C. *America's Longest War: The United States and Vietnam, 1950–1975.* 2nd ed. New York: McGraw-Hill, 1986.

Hunt, Richard A. *Pacification: The American Struggle for Vietnam's Hearts and Minds.* Boulder, CO: Westview, 1995.

McKenna, Thomas P. *Kontum: The Battle to Save South Vietnam,* Lexington: University Press of Kentucky, 2011.

McNamara, Robert S. *In Retrospect: The Tragedy and Lessons of Vietnam.* With Brian VanDeMark. New York: Random House, 1995.

Nguyen, Viet Thanh. *Nothing Ever Dies: Vietnam and the Memory of War.* Cambridge, MA: Harvard University Press, 2016.

Nighswonger, William A. *Rural Pacification in Vietnam.* New York: Praeger, 1966.

Sheehan, Neil. *A Bright Shining Lie: John Paul Vann and America in Vietnam.* New York: Random House, 1988.

Snepp, Frank. *Decent Interval: An Insider's Account of Saigon's Indecent End.* New York: Random House, 1977.

Spector, Ronald H. *After Tet: The Bloodiest Year in Vietnam.* New York: Free Press, 1993.

Tran, Dinh Tho. *Pacification.* Washington, D.C.: U.S. Army Center of Military History, 1980.

Journal Articles

Bullington, J.R. "Assessing Pacification in Vietnam: We Won the Counterinsurgency War!" *Small Wars Journal* (smallwarsjournal.com) (March 23, 2012).

Fritz, Carl R. "An American Civilian in the Vietnam War." In *American Diplomacy,* 1996. http://www.unc.edu/depts/diplomat/AD_Issues/Amdipl_2/Fritz.html.

Hohn, Mandy, Farrah Meisel, Jacleen Mowery, and Jennifer Smith. With contributions from Minhye Ha. "A Legacy of Vietnam: The Lessons of CORDS." Fort Leavenworth, KS: Col. Arthur D. Simons Center for the Study of Interagency Cooperation, *InterAgency Journal* 2, no. 2 (Summer 2011).

Jenson, Richard Jenson. *Vietnam War Bibliography.* http://www.americanhistory projects.com/downloads/vietnam.htm.

Bibliography

Pinard, Matthew Douglas. "The American and South Vietnamese Pacification Efforts During the Vietnam War." Master's thesis, Louisiana State University, 2002. http://digitalcommons.lsu.edu/gradschool_theses/2732.

Schoux, William P. " The Vietnam Experience: A Model of Successful Civil-Military Partnership?" pdf.USAID.gov, 2004.

Thompson, Robert John, III. "More Sieve Than Shield: The U.S. Army and CORDS in the Pacification of Phu Yen Province, Republic of Vietnam, 1965–1972." PhD diss., University of Southern Mississippi, 2016.

Index

Index

Index